Ritual in Industrial Society
A Sociological Analysis of Ritualism in Modern England

Ritual in Industrial Society

A Sociological Analysis of Ritualism in Modern England

by Robert Bocock

Distributed in the United States by
CRANE, RUSSAK & COMPANY, INC.
347 Madison Avenue
New York, New York 10017

ISBN 0 04 300044 4

Printed in Great Britain
in 11 point Plantin type
by T. & A. Constable Ltd,
Hopetoun Street, Edinburgh

Originally and naturally, sexual pleasure was the good, the beautiful, the happy, that which united man with nature in general. When sexual feelings and religious feelings become separated from one another, that which is sexual was forced to become the bad, the infernal, the diabolical.

Wilhelm Reich
The Mass Psychology of Fascism
(Farrar, Straus and Giroux, New York 1970)
p. 148.

Preface

Ritual is concerned with the process of either binding people's feelings into the existing organisation of society, or with aiding them to become critical and independent of it. This book is concerned with seeing how ritual action aids or prevents social change at both a political level and a more personal level. Such concerns arise particularly from the work of those social thinkers who have tried to relate ideas developed by Freud to the wider concerns of sociology. Norman Brown, Herbert Marcuse, Wilhelm Reich, and Erich Fromm particularly, have tried to develop the more sociological aspects of psycho-analysis, and their work has influenced this analysis of ritual in indirect, but fundamental, ways.

The choice of the area itself assumes that in ritual people are doing something significant which sociologists should seek to understand and eventually build into their models of industrial societies. Non-psycho-analytic and pre-psycho-analytic perspectives in sociology do not focus on such non-rational areas of action to any great extent. Nor do they give much weight to such phenomena in their models of how societies remain stable over time, or in their identification of the agents of change in modern societies.

A more psycho-analytic sociology, however, would make conscious and unconscious feelings, desires, wishes, and symbols central to understanding man's behaviour in societies. The focus on the human body, on the sexual drives in men and women of all ages, and on people's knowledge of the eventual death of the body, saves such a perspective from being 'over-idealist' in the Marxist sense, and from being 'over-abstract' about people in the way some Marxists are.

Ritual has been chosen for special attention because it is in such activities that desires, feelings, symbols and wishes are handled and related to the groups and institutions, from the family to the state, of which the individual is a member, and which make up what is called a 'society'.

The analyses in this book, however, are not dogmatically psycho-analytical. The experiences of people as they themselves have reported them are given more validity than a dogmatic approach usually allows. Categories of analysis cannot be imposed dogmatically on to experience, they must be developed from an understanding of, and a respect for, people's own ways of describing their experiences. This is so because otherwise there is no way of controlling empirically what can be said within a particular sociological perspective. This is not to say that sociologists should have no categories of their own for a more systematic and cumulative understanding of action than any one person, or group, needs. Such a completely unanalytical, non-categorising, approach becomes impossible to maintain in the analysis of historical power structures and the part rituals may play in maintaining or changing them.

My thanks are due to the students and staff at Brunel University, especially in the Departments of Sociology and Psychology, who have helped generate what has been for me a lively and creative intellectual atmosphere, not least because psychoanalytic ideas were discussed seriously. Many clergy, religious people, and workers in the theatre, have been very helpful in providing time to talk to me about ritual. Students and staff of the Richmond Fellowship have been of great help too.

Special acknowledgements and thanks are due to Professor Elliott Jaques, and to Professors Mary Douglas and David Martin, for valuable discussions at various points in the development of this book. June Montgomery, Susan Verney, Richard Legg, John Wickens, Janet Mattinson, and Jean Bocock gave invaluable help in discussions and encouragement to work on the area of ritual action. None of them, of course, are responsible for errors of fact or of interpretation, for these will be my own. Brenda Legget struggled with the typing of the manuscript, for which many thanks are due.

R. B.

Contents

Illustrations

Introduction

To analyse ritual action in industrial society turned out to be a large task when it was broken down into separate parts, and much larger than can be dealt with in one book. For once one starts looking for ritual action it is amazing how much there is— hand-shaking, teeth cleaning, taking medicines, car riding, eating, entertaining guests, drinking tea, or coffee, beer, sherry, whisky, etc., taking a dog for a walk, watching television, going to the cinema, listening to records, visiting relatives, routines at work, singing at work, children's street games, hunting and so on.[1] One can go adding activities *ad infinitum*, and still stretch the definition of ritual to include them all. Some restrictions become necessary if ritual is to be a meaningful concept, with some kind of boundary.

The first task is to reach some definition of the term 'ritual'. Some anthropologists and sociologists use 'ritual' to refer to symbolic action with a reference to supernatural beings. They may use 'ceremony' to describe secular rituals.[2] Here the term ritual is used to cover both religious ritual and other types of ritual, which might be called 'ceremonies' by others. The only thing that is of some importance in this matter of terminology is to be clear whether the subject matter is restricted to religion, in a narrow sense or not. In this book there is discussion of religious, political, aesthetic and life-cycle rituals.

The main ritual actions of England are still very much connected with the nationally established Church, both at a local level, and at the level of the whole society, as a nation-state. These ritual actions are still used by many people in the population; the estimates vary of how many claim to be members of the Church of England, depending on how membership is established, but it is about two-thirds of the English population on the basis of self-ascription, which is as good a method as any of gaining a figure for membership of such a Church.[3] To ignore such ritual as goes on in England and to concentrate on more fashionable ritual action such as occurs in minority sects of Christianity and in Eastern religions, or trendy theatrical rituals, is tempting, but not the best method of gaining understanding of ritual action in a society such as England, where little is known about the role of the more basic rituals in people's lives. The central ritual events of the nation and the local community, as well as the life-cycle rituals of the individual, all still involve some reference to the national Church. This relationship is a problematic one. It seems to be fundamental though, and cannot be ignored even if at first sight it seems duller and less interesting than some other rituals might appear, both to sociologists and to the general reader.

Some importance is given at the beginning of the book to various theoretical approaches to the phenomenon of ritual in human societies, as this is essential in order to be able to identify the key areas in ritual action. The central problem here concerns how the sociologist is to know the *meaning* of ritual actions.[4] Descriptive case studies which lack a theoretical orientation are not much help, because they are difficult for other researchers to use in comparative work if they are not guided by a similar basic approach.[5]

In sociology there is little agreement on basic approaches to ritual action, especially in assessing its importance in industrial societies. Sociologists have usually assumed that secularisation has increased, is increasing, and will continue to increase, under industrial conditions. As a consequence sociologists and others, including some clergy, have assumed that ritual action has declined in importance in urban, industrial conditions. This assumption has only recently been examined systematically within sociology.

The main assumption here is that ritual is more important in industrial societies than has been usually thought. It may well turn out after empirical study that industrial workers are not as unritualised as some theories hold they should be. For other groups in industrial societies, especially some of the youth and old people, ritual is of central importance in their lives, whether it takes the form of prayer, meditation, or attendance at religious or aesthetic rituals. The way ritual action is regarded in a society, or group, gives the sociologist some ideas about the quality of group life, and the ways in which the group relates to the body, to symbols, to feelings, to the *non-rational area of life*. This has been under-studied because it is assumed that rational action is more typical, and more important, in industrial societies than non-rational action. This assumption is challenged in the theoretical discussion and carried over into the more empirical analysis later in the book.

The theoretical discussion is indispensable in a work on ritual in industrial society to show the basis for using, or not using, as the case may be, the work of anthropologists on ritual, which has been developed in relation to rural, agricultural societies. After this, the way in which ritual is structured in an industrial society will be analysed. Finally, new developments in ritual in industrial societies will be examined, in the light of the earlier discussion, and in terms of their relation to social change and the counter-culture.

Chapter One

'Man Shall Not Live By Bread Alone'

VIEWS OF MAN IN THE SOCIOLOGICAL ANALYSIS OF
RITUAL

There is within sociology, and certainly outside that discipline,
some scepticism about the importance of the study of sociology
of religion and of ritual. This view rests on a hard-headed
political and economic view of human societies, which sees
religion as important only when it has political, or economic,
consequences for a given society. For example, C. Wright Mills,
writing about what he calls the 'master symbols of legitimation'
says, 'Such symbols, however, do not form some autonomous
realm within a society; their social relevance lies in their use to
justify or oppose the arrangement of power and the positions
within this arrangement of the powerful.'[1]

This approach to the place of symbols, which would in many
societies be religious, is of relevance for sociology, especially a
sociology geared to the relevant political issues of our era. But
is it all sociology should be concerned with, in its analysis of
religion? There are a number of reasons for answering 'No' to
this question. Firstly, it fails to do justice to the fact that large
numbers of people in the modern world's societies are influenced
in their lives by religious beliefs, symbols, rituals and values in
ways which have little to do, at first sight, with politics or
economics. Religion is for many a crucial dimension of life, but
one which is best conceptualised by the sociologist at the outset
of analysis as being *sui generis*, a dimension not reducible to any
other. The meaning of life to many people is interfused with
religion. Such a statement may appear to be unprovable, but
there is some empirical evidence for it from surveys of religious
opinions in advanced industrial societies.[2]

Secondly, from the point of view of major social change, changes in religion have been of some importance not just for political élites and ruling classes, but for other groups in societies. This is not to assert that religion is the only cause of change, but to call attention to the role religion can play in change in a way similar to that of Max Weber. This would seem to be especially true of change in relation to the 'quality of life' in given periods and in specific societies.[3] Such change is not necessarily in either a desirable or undesirable direction; the influence of positivism still tends to operate uncritically in this area, however, among those who seem to assume that the decline of religion is to be welcomed. An alternative view is equally possible; to say that the quality of life would improve for many people by a recovery of the sacred, of the 'holy', dimension in their lives. This view could be held by clergy, and even by social scientists, especially those in the Jungian tradition.[4] Initially, however, a sociology of religion would be neutral on this issue. However, in the long run such value judgements will emerge in a sociologist's work. This is because the study of Sociology of Religion raises the central issue about the role of theories of the nature of man in sociology more than any other area within sociology. The crux of any analysis of religion comes when religion is treated as the independent variable, if this is even done. Much sociology has shown very well the ways in which social stratification, politics, economics, influence religion, but often the analyses miss out the role played by religious consciousness itself.[5] The problem is not simple, for how one conducts an analysis in sociology of religion will reflect a judgement about the role of religious consciousness in human beings; either that it is basically illusory and masks the real problems of life in society, or that it is the only way in which men can make their lives basically meaningful and satisfying. People tend to be drawn to one or other of these perspectives; it is exceptionally difficult to remain neutral on such a central issue.

Sociologists, nevertheless, have to come to some working judgement on this issue. Religion is to be treated here as a basic non-reducible dimension in human experience. The symbolic, the sacred, the holy, the mythic, the poetic, whatever it is called, it is difficult to operate with a view of man which leaves this area out, as of no significance to modern man.[6] This is not to say everyone has such experiences, or even that a majority do. Rather it is to say that religious consciousness is significant in human societies as we know them, and that it therefore must have some place in any view about man-in-society.

People seek some dimension to existence in addition to the utilitarian basis of everyday living, once the economy is capable of yielding an acceptable standard of living for them. Religions, and some ideologies, provide this for many groups in industrial societies, especially through the ritual actions of the group, not primarily through the intellectual level. The arts, 'pop', and sports also provide this dimension, by providing drama through identification with 'stars' in the entertainment world and in sport, and through identification with a group wider than the normal membership groups of the people concerned. Spectacle and excitement are provided by these means, as well as by political and military ceremonials.

How are such spectacles and entertainments to be regarded? There is an attitude held by some liberal rationalists towards nearly all rituals and ceremonials which sees them as unnecessary and unfortunate. They are unnecessary for mature, adult people, and they are unfortunate in that the basis of their appeal is emotional, and not intellectual. This assessment of ritual derives from a view of human beings which is not adequate in the light of what social scientists know of people in many different cultures and historical periods, and it is a view which is to be challenged here. The alternative view of man is summed up in the well-known biblical phrase 'Man shall not live by bread alone' (Matthew 4:4). Man is a symbol-producing animal; he can set up systems of meaning in terms of which to experience his life. Susanne Langer has shown this more clearly, and her view is expressed in the following: 'This basic need, which certainly is obvious only in man, is *the need of symbolisation*. The symbol-making function is one of man's primary activities, like eating, looking, or moving about.'[7] Models of man which do not take this capacity seriously into account will be seen to be faulty, especially in the way they handle, or fail to handle, the part played by ritual action in human society, including modern, industrial societies.

Man is more than a 'naked ape', more than a complex computer on legs, more than a behavioural organism of an elaborate type.[8] These views of man are held by many people because they are thought to be scientific, but an adequate scientific theory of man must include his unique capacity for producing symbols, for making his life meaningful, and even dramatic, in the sense that he sees himself as part of a larger story, a larger drama. It is not that the hard-headed views of man are wholly mistaken, it is that they are too limited to cope with all that we know about men living in societies.

We do not know scientifically that all culture and all religion is a defence against 'reality'; nor that matter is more 'real' than human consciousness. What is called 'matter' has produced man, his consciousness and its products. It is not possible to single out one element as more basic and 'real' and then analyse everything to do with consciousness in terms of this 'matter'. Perhaps so many do this as a reaction against the alternative error of analysing everything from the assumption that the 'spirit' or consciousness is more real than matter. We need a more monistic view of man-in-the-world than either of these. Both 'matter' and 'consciousness' exist, and are interrelated. Neither is reducible to the other.[9]

Ritual raises problems also of the relation of the rational scientific mode of understanding to the non-rational mode of perception which lies at the root of religion and art, and their associated rituals. Is the aim of such a scientific understanding to increase man's rational control over his non-rational parts? Is it to further the goals of the Enlightenment, to enable reason to control the passions? Or is it rather to seek to understand ritual action, and its role in social life, to aid integration of body and mind, intellect and unconscious symbols?

A sociological understanding of ritual action can aid the development of a more integrated view of man as a being with an intellect, but also with a body, and a capacity for producing symbols. The intellectual activity of developing such understanding of ritual action is therefore conceived of as itself part of this process. It must never become a substitute for actual lived participation in ritual action; but it may be that some of the 'ritual specialists', both performers and 'audiences', may be aided by a sociological perspective on their life's work.

METHODOLOGICAL AND PHILOSOPHICAL PRESUPPOSITIONS

Although sociologists and other social scientists are usually very careful to distinguish their analytical and empirical work from value judgements, which in this case includes ontological as well as ethical value judgements, some believers may be right in thinking many social scientists really think there is little point in any sort of judgement other than their scientific ones. They are seen to be committed to 'science', their belief system may be called 'Positivism'.

For non-positivistic social scientists, there is then a special problem—what is to be the relation between social science and commitments in the rest of life? It is possible to subordinate sociology to these extra-commitments, as do some dogmatic Marxists and some Christian sociologists. This, however, seems unsatisfactory when judged as knowledge which can be useful to attain the very ends and values posited by the belief system and value system itself. This style of sociology can become a closed belief system; one which comes close to being based on wish-fulfilment, for the beliefs and assertions are not checked against what can only be called 'real life'.

In sociology, which is removed from any real value commitments, we are left with research which is in fact implicitly informed by the values of powerful status groups in the society; it is not really neutral. Its neutrality leads to triviality, in that any really interesting and important issues will be ones in which values are inextricably involved. This is the case with some sociology of religion. Either the subject is seen as one in which religion is exposed as false consciousness (dogmatic Marxism) or as a subject useful to élites in the Churches (Christian sociology).[10] Alternatively, it becomes devoted to counting who goes to church, how often, and with what beliefs, using material gathered from opinion polls. In all these cases no analytical or theoretical questions are really posed, for either the answers are known in advance, or they are seen as non-questions.

Analytically based sociology, tackling alive issues, is not value neutral in any simplistic sense. It is not a question of espousing one set of values and beliefs against another, but of choosing problems and tackling them in ways which are very much influenced by values.

Ritual action, the problem chosen for this book, is related to value concerns. Rituals are undervalued in advanced industrial society by technological and managerial élites, although in such societies many sub-groups are dedicated to ritual action. Technological, rationalist, ideology is nevertheless anti-ritual. This book is conceived as redressing the balance somewhat, towards more positive approaches to ritual.

Rituals relate to key areas of our lives—to our sense of community or lack of it; to social cohesion or social conflict; to the human body, death, birth, illness, health, sexuality; and to symbols of beauty and holiness.

Some groups are, however, reaching a new awareness of the importance of ritual for human beings to relate to one another in the heights and depths of experience. Some parts of the youth culture, some religious groups, some in the theatre and other arts are aware of this.[11] Serious sociological study and analysis of ritual action is worthwhile to enable us to see what can be done, under what conditions, to deepen our experience of ourselves, our bodies, and of one another.

As used in this book, 'religion' has a limited meaning, namely social action which relates to symbols which express the 'holy', or the 'numinous' as Rudolf Otto calls it.[12] Some people operating with other definitions could see all the rituals, of all types to be examined here, as religious.[13] If it is said religion means to bind together, then much of the civic and political ritual action could be called religious. The beautiful and the holy, as categories, overlap at some points, and thus some would claim that much artistic expression is really religious.

One can ask what are the consequences of religious ritual as defined here. This will have to be examined in more detail in the chapter on religious ritual, but it is worth pointing out that one of the most important ideas is that experience of the holy, the sacred, can lead to the introduction of novelty, freshness, into our existence. This point is worth stressing because in our culture at the present time, the holy as a concept does not suggest this to many people. It seems a highly tradition-bound area of human experience, and is even somewhat drab; it is certainly not often perceived as being the bearer of newness and freshness into our lives. It is for this reason that Otto's concept of the 'numinous' is so useful for sociology, because it has no such connotations. It is possible to see what is meant by saying that people who have had experience of the 'numinous', for instance from drugs, or from more traditional methods of devotion, find their whole life-experiences reinvigorated and refreshed, at least for a while.

A central assumption in the analysis in this book is that religious experience must be allowed, analytically, by the sociologist as a possible type of experience, and not always analysed as basically or 'really' about something else.

A distinction is necessary between the phenomenology and the ontology of religion. A phenomenological analysis of religious experience would show the type of experiences which people in particular cultures call experience of 'the holy', or numinous, but would 'bracket off' to use Husserl's term, questions of ontology.[14] It is relevant to ask what people themselves believe ontologically, for instance what they would count as an experience of a supernatural reality 'God'. But just as the sociologist is not called upon, *qua* sociologist, to accept this belief as ontologically valid, nor is it part of his task to develop his own ontology about the 'reality' underlying religious experiences. Indeed, the point can be put more strongly—it is impossible for the sociologist to do any ontological speculation within his frame of reference. The point can be made with relation to the sociology of art, and it is worth doing this to show the logic of the position being maintained here, in an area which many people find less problematic than that of religion. Phenomenology could attempt to describe types of aesthetic experience—what it is to listen and to play music, or to watch dancing, or to paint, read a novel, see a film or play. A sociologist could ask people who do these things frequently, what they think they are doing and experiencing. People might or might not be able to give coherent statements about their beliefs in respect of aesthetic experience; some might think they communicate with the basic structure of the universe, others that they contact their psyches, or the collective unconscious, or even God, or gods. These beliefs are analytically and empirically separate from the aesthetic experience itself. There are fewer ontologies in sociology surrounding aesthetic experience, and fewer reductionist perspectives—that art is really about the 'society'. 'Aesthetic experience' is an analytical category of experience in its own right, although types of aesthetic experience can be examined in relation to different social, political, economic structures without reductionism.[15] The same is possible with religious experience; it is distinct as an analytical type from aesthetic, political, sexual, experiences, and yet equally necessary to have a complete range of types of human experience as a basis for sociology, anthropology and psychology.

It is worth examining briefly, at this point, some of the outstanding social scientists' work on religion to see how their basic ontological assumptions affect their view of ritual, particularly. They claimed to be developing a scientific view of religion, but their analyses turn on assumptions which belong to the philosophy of positivism and materialism, but not strictly to science as such.

Emile Durkheim's work is based on positivistic assumptions, both in regard to method and metaphysical assumptions. It is, however, in certain key respects, self-contradictory on religion. Durkheim wants to respect the experience of worshippers in their claims of experiencing something more powerful than themselves, something awesome. And yet his positivism leads him to claim that this is really an experience of society, the group consciousness. Beneath this lies an important claim and insight, namely that people's experience is dependent on groups, on other people and on communicating with them. It is, in other words, properly sociological, and not psychologistic and individualistic. Religious experience is dependent on religious groups and their cultures; it does not arise initially from within an isolated psyche. The contradiction in Durkheim is that he confuses the conditions necessary for religious experience with the content of the experience. His analysis of the sacred is powerful and shows an understanding of the content of religious experience; but he is unable to leave the analysis there and goes on to show that in the light of the ontology he accepts, as a positivist, that the sacred *is* society in some reified form.

But from our point of view, religion ceases to be an inexplicable hallucination and takes a foothold in reality. In fact, we can say that the believer is not deceived when he believes in the existence of a moral power upon which he depends and from which he receives all that is best in himself: this power exists, it is society. When the Australian is carried outside himself and feels a new life flowing within him whose intensity surprises him, he is not the dupe of an illusion; this exaltation is real and is really the effect of forces outside of and superior to the individual. It is true that he is wrong in thinking that this increase of vitality is the work of a power in the form of some animal or plant. But this error is merely in regard to the letter of the symbol by which this being is represented to the mind, and the external appearance which the imagination has given it, and not in regard to the fact of its existence. Behind these figures and metaphors be they gross or refined, there is a concrete and living reality. Thus religion acquires a meaning and a reasonableness that the most intransigent rationalist cannot misunderstand. Its primary object is not to give men a representation of the physical world; for if that were its essential task, we could not understand how it has been able to survive, for, on this side, it is scarcely more than a fabric of errors. Before all, it is a system of ideas with which the individuals represent to themselves the society of which they are members and the obscure but intimate relations which they have with it. This is its primary function; and though metaphorical and symbolic, this representation is not unfaithful. Quite on the contrary, it translates everything essential in the relations which are to be explained; for it is an eternal truth that outside of us there exists something greater than us, with which we enter into communion.

That is why we can rest assured in advance that the practices of the cult, whatever they may be, are something more than movements without importance and gestures without efficacy.[16]

Freud also made ontological judgements about the object of religious experience, seeing religious ideas as entirely the product of men's own psychological needs and wishes, within an entirely negative framework of assumptions about the consequences of religion for men and culture. Phillip Rieff argues that he failed to see the positive and potentially creative aspects of religious experience.[17] Nevertheless, Freud's analysis has contributed to our understanding of some religious experience and behaviour, but it would seem best to bear in mind that he confuses scientific analysis with ontology, and thus does not always provide a description of religious experience as it would seem to the worshipper and believer—the terms he uses to describe such experience derive from his theory, with all its ontological assumptions. Religion is illusion, albeit a collective one, not an individual one.[18] Ritual is obsessive action, though it is collective and is distinct in this respect from the obsessive acts of neurotics. The obsessive actions and prohibitions of neurotics are based on instinctual renunciations, largely of the sexual instinct. Those of religion are also based on the renunciation of instinctual impulses, but in this case not just of the sexual impulses, but also those of self-seeking anti-social impulses. Here Freud is seeing religion as making some contribution to the maintanance of social life. He also recognises the symbolic content of religious ritual, and its fullness and significance when compared with the obsessions of neurotics which at first might seem pointless.

It is easy to see where the resemblances lie between neurotic ceremonials and the sacred acts of religious ritual; in the qualms of conscience brought on by their neglect, in their complete isolation from all other actions (shown in the prohibition against interruption) and in the conscientiousness with which they are carried out in every detail. But the differences are equally obvious, and a few of them are so glaring as to make the comparison a sacrilege; the greater individual variability of (neurotic) ceremonial actions in contrast to the stereotyped character of rituals (prayer, turning to the East, etc.), their private nature as opposed to the public and communal character of religious observances, above all, however, the fact that, while the minutiae of religious ceremonial are full of significance and have a symbolic meaning, those of neurotics seem foolish and senseless. In this respect an obsessional neurosis presents a travesty, half comic and half tragic, of a private religion . . .[19]

This is one of Freud's more positive statements about religion, and is different in tone from *The Future of an Illusion*. Much of his work on religion is highly influenced by the Judeo-Christian ideas of God as a father, and his theories, especially in *Moses and Monotheism*, are highly speculative. They turn on the killing of the primitive father, and the ensuing emotional consequences for mankind. Freud said almost nothing of the applicability of his theory to Eastern religions, which have less of a father-figure image of a transcendent God. Freud's ontology, which is that of a nineteenth-century, or early twentieth-century, scientific materialist, with his own unique additions about the historical truth of the killing of the primitive father, continually interferes with his analyses of religion. He describes reality as 'hostile life' (in *The Future of an Illusion*). Yet how can he know scientifically that life is hostile; can his pessimism about man be supported scientifically? Surely no; he has confused his own ontology about the nature of man-in-the-world with the act of scientific analysis of religion and ritual. Yet his work remains seminal for such analysis when his own belief system is to some extent removed from it.

Carl Jung had an acute awareness of the problem of meaning, and the attempts to formulate viable answers to it in the wide variety of human cultures of which we know. It is this which can be seen to be at the centre of Jung's psychology. 'Among all my patients in the second half of life—that is to say over 35—there has not been one whose problem in the last resort was not that of finding a religious outlook on life.' And 'A psycho-neurosis must be understood as the suffering of a human being who has not discovered what life means for him. . . . The patient is looking for something that will take possession of him and give meaning and form to the confusion of his neurotic mind.'[20]

In the Jungian tradition, as it has developed, there has been a lot of attention paid to myth, symbols and dreams. The task of relating people to their bodies has been less stressed; the realm of the Unconscious is almost as disembodied as that of the rational consciousness. Thus ritual has never really been at the centre of Jungian concern, except in so far as it relates to myth.[21] Ritual has a more central focus here in so far as it involves the use of the body—and if 'ritual' connotes a somewhat slow, unphysical set of stereotyped movements, it should be remembered that the category includes dancing. The use of the body, together with visual and aural symbols, places ritual at the centre of attention if our concern is with the split in our culture between the body and the mind; the non-rational and the over-rational.

Clearly, the 'unconscious' is very much connected with the body and its desires and needs, but the connection can tend, in Jungian writing, to get underplayed.[22] Nevertheless, Jung does provide a much less scientistic view of religion in general, and is less reductionist than Freud. Jung's work does contain an ontology, one which is more compatible with those of the world religions than that of Freud. Potentially, it is fruitful for the analysis of religious and aesthetic ritual, and Jung's theory of the stages of man is useful in relation to life-cycle ritual. The fact that Jung claimed to find a collective element in his analyses of unconscious material does mean that his theory and work has an immediate connection with a more sociological orientation than the more rigorist individualism of some Freudians.

Freud, however, remains firmly rooted to the body through sexuality and death (Eros and Thanatos), which he stresses more than Jung.

It has been said earlier that what has to be explained in a social scientific theory depends on a whole set of assumptions which derive from a more fundamental philosophical anthropology about man-in-the-world.[23] Levi-Strauss makes the process of providing a scientific explanation central to his thinking and thus attempts to build a theory which will meet such a set of criteria. By doing so, he is forced to make 'intellect' primary, and to see structures as basic in human cultures, which then cause the feelings of people. He writes, 'Actually, impulses and emotions explain nothing; they are always results, either of the power of the body or of the impotence of the mind. In both cases they are consequences, never causes. . . .'[24]

The structuralist view of man which is implicit in the work of Levi-Strauss, is that feelings and emotions are highly distinct from intellect, and intellectual processes. Feelings and emotions are seen to derive from culture—a point Levi-Strauss makes in *Totemism*—in a very strict way:

> Men do not act, as members of a group, in accordance with what each feels as an individual; each man feels as a function of the way in which he is permitted or obliged to act. Customs are given as external norms before giving rise to internal senti-ments, and these non-sentient norms determine the sentiments of individuals as well as the circumstances in which they may, or must, be displayed.[25]

It seems only the intellect is relatively free from these con-straints. Even it is subject to 'structures'. The problem with this view is its rigorous divorce of feelings and emotions from the processes of the intellect. Basically it perpetuates the 'rationality versus feelings' split of much Western thought. At a lower level of analysis the point made by Levi-Strauss, that feelings are programmed by cultures, may be true of simple societies, but seems not to be true of complex industrial society where people are much more individualised. Nor is there one clear culture with one set, or even a limited set, of permitted emotions and feelings, for there are many sub-cultures and new ones are created by groups who feel out of place in some of the major sub-cultures. There is also a danger in Levi-Strauss of a renewal of what Dennis Wrong called 'the over-socialised conception of man.'[26]

Levi-Strauss' notion of 'untamed thought' which is a constant in all human social life, not the thought of primitive and archaic peoples, is of importance for ritual behaviour and action.[27] It entails the assumption that ritual will still reflect structures which men have always developed. This is to be treated as a hypothesis, not taken as an *a priori* truth. It suggests that there are constant elements in human thought and symbols, in that there are constant structures developed by man. The problem with structuralism becomes clear if we ask why we want to explain anything in social science; if it is to gain the most abstract, formalised knowledge possible about a particular phenomenon, with a view to simply knowing, then to concentrate on structures seems to aid in the attainment of this goal. If knowledge is to be *used*, then the meaning of action, its subjective side in people's consciousness, becomes more important. This is because it is more near to lived experience. It is interesting to note Piaget here.

Structures are not just simply convenient theoretical constructs; they exist apart from the anthropologist, for they are the source of the relations he observes; a structure would lose all truth value if it did not have this direct connection with the facts. But neither are they transcendent essences, for Levi-Strauss is not a phenomenologist and denies the primacy of the 'me' or the 'lived'. The recurrent formula is that structures 'emanate from the intellect', from the human mind as ever the same;. . .[28]

Pursuit of knowledge in a formal science has an appeal to some, but not most people, for most want to know how to live their lives; their interest in science is in its consequences for living—how to stay well, and to be happier. Structuralism may be something of a new departure; but as yet in Levi-Strauss, it remains over-idealist in the Kantian sense—seeking basic categories underlying change and difference. Or it can become highly deterministic, thus loosing the gains of what Talcott Parsons called 'the voluntaristic theory of action'. Experienced meaning is lost or discounted, in favour of formalism, and more universal 'structures'.

The analysis of religion in Karl Marx's and Engels' writings is related to their ontological position as dialectical materialists.[29]

Much of their analysis of Christianity in capitalist societies is useful as a starting point for sociological, empirical analysis. For instance, churches in the nineteenth century did teach a conservative conformist philosophy to their congregations of all social classes. However, Marx's and Engels' basic lack of understanding of religious experience, partly because it was seen as merely subjective, and partly because it was seen by Marx and Engels to be about an unreal world, makes their analysis of religion one-sided, and lacking in depth and awareness of the range and variety of such experience. Many contemporary social scientists share their lack of empathy with religion as a dimension of humanity's life experience, even though most of them are not Marxists. It is part of the same prejudice that sees economics and politics as basic to human social life, and symbolic needs as secondary. Yet what we know of man should lead to a view of human beings as a complex of needs, but not to one in which one set of needs is seen as more fundamental than another set, whether it is the symbolic, or the economic or the biological needs which are taken as primary. If any one of these aspects of man is ignored or undeveloped, then we do not have what we normally call a 'human'.

The work of Marx and Engels will be important later in the book, and so further discussion of their ideas is left until then.

Similarly, with the work of Max Weber, which is of such importance for modern sociology of religion, discussion of his ideas will occur in later chapters. Suffice to say here that Weber's sociology of religion is an advance on that of the others so far considered, because he did keep a clear distinction between developing an ontology, and a view of religion based on such an ontology, from doing a sociological analysis of religious experience in various historical periods and types of society.[30] He was able to take the subjective meaning people themselves gave to their religious experience as an important element in his analysis, as for instance in his classic essay on '*The Protestant Ethic and the Spirit of Capitalism*'.[31] Yet this did not exclude taking historical and social structural factors into his analysis too, as is the case with some more recent phenomenological analyses. His approach is, therefore, of great importance for this

C

work, in that his methodological presuppositions have influenced those used here. They are not identical, though, for Weber remains pre-Freudian in his work on religion. He does not see religion and art as two very important social institutions for the expression of unconscious life, for relating men and women with this part of themselves. He tends to see the non-rational as disappearing in modern society, rather than as being changed in form, but still very much present, as it was in other historical periods. He assumed that the growth of rational action in modern European society would entail the decrease of the non-rational in human lives. This is not so. We can now see, since Freud, that even the most rational types of action have non-rational sources. This does not necessarily reduce their rationality. But it does mean that the non-rational in human life has not simply disappeared. It is still at work in modern man.

In a theory of ritual action one can look for a view of man, based on an examination of a crucial area of human action, which seems to involve all of man—his body, feelings, his social relationships, his culture, and his intellect too. The relationship of such a theory of ritual action to a philosophical anthropology is complex. It is not meant to prove in any simple way higher-level statements about man-in-the-world; rather it can suggest something about this by illustrating how different assumptions about philosophical anthropology affect our understanding of ritual, what is seen as problematic and in need of some kind of explanation, and what is not. By so doing it can affect the development of a growing picture of man-in-the-world being developed by philosophy, and the social and natural sciences concerned with man.

Chapter Two

Towards a Sociology of Ritual Action

In the course of a year, a person in a modern industrial society will participate in a very large number of rituals. Some of these are being shared by many others in the same society, such as Christmas Day, or an event such as the Cup Final. Others are shared by fewer people such as a birthday, but they occur regularly. Still others take place infrequently in any person's life such as weddings, or funerals, but are widespread ritual events common to nearly all members of the population.

There are also ritual events of a less widespread character, which specialised groups watch, or are involved in performing, for instance many of the arts and sports are of this kind. Then there are the ritual events of various organisations in the society, such as schools, colleges, hospitals, offices, factories, the army, navy and air force, and those of the churches and other religious groups. Thus, in modern industrial societies, there is a large amount and a great variety of ritual action which may seem surprising to those who tend to think of ritual as belonging to 'primitive society' and not industrial ones.

However, some people would agree that there is a large amount of what might be called 'ritual' in industrial societies, yet they would argue that it is not very significant in the lives of most people in such societies. In this sense it is seen as a leftover from more traditional societies in feudal Europe, but not as a dynamic element in modern society. People in many spheres of work, from some clergy to social scientists and politicians, often make the assumption that industrial societies are *secular* and are growing more secular with each decade that passes. The assumption is made also, that secular society is society with very little ritual. David Martin has shown that the assumption of secularisation is one which can be challenged both theoretically and empirically;[1] and Mary Douglas has pointed out that there is no justification for assuming that 'primitive' societies are necessarily ritualised and highly religious, for there are 'secular primitives', just as there are 'religious moderns'.[2] But quite apart from this, it is not the case that, in any society, ritual is all necessarily 'religious', for much of it occurs outside spheres normally thought of as religious, certainly in cultures influenced by Western conceptions of religion. For example, dance of all kinds can be seen as ritual action, yet the Christian Church has not usually allowed dancing as part of ritual action in the worship of God.[3]

So far the term 'ritual' has been used to refer to events which nearly everyone would agree were to be called ritual, although some might be doubtful about specific cases, such as calling dancing, or sporting events, 'ritual'. Obviously in order to decide such issues it is not possible to avoid some discussion of the definition of 'ritual'. Simply expressed, 'ritual' is to be used here to mean *bodily action in relation to symbols*. The action is *social*, that is it involves groups of people who share some sets of expectations in common; it is not primarily individual action, although some of this derives its meaning from group action, yet is performed in private, for example, praying. Notice also the word 'action' is used; this is to distinguish ritual actions from what ethologists and biologists might term ritual *behaviour*.[4] The difference is that in ritual behaviour, the animal or person attaches no subjective meaning to the act; it is a learned habit which is repeated frequently, in a stereotyped form. This sort of ritual behaviour is not related to symbols. The use of the term 'symbol' follows that of Susanne Langer:

> . . . as soon as an expressive act is performed without inner momentary compulsion it is no longer self-expressive; it is expressive in the logical sense. It is not a sign of the emotion it conveys, but a symbol of it; instead of completing the natural history of a feeling, it denotes the feeling and may merely bring it to mind, even for the actor. When an action acquires such a meaning it becomes a gesture.[5]

Ritual is the symbolic use of bodily movement and gesture in a social situation to express and articulate meaning.

Ritual can integrate bodily feelings and emotions with rational social purposes, and can thus go some way to healing the splits between the body and the intellect. Without rituals life becomes utilitarian, technocratic and cold, devoid of human emotions. Alternatively, rituals may be rejected in the name of a more spontaneous approach to human feelings and emotional expression, encouraging passionate outbursts of feelings as the only genuinely human way of feeling. Some elements of the youth counter-culture approach this position.[6] Rituals relate people to their bodies in ways which few other social actions do, for they involve using the body to express feelings, and even ideas, in a disciplined way.

Social groups in any given society use rituals for their own ends and purposes, however. Ritual has been used, and still is, as an effective way of socialising people to conform to values and ways of life which they have not chosen for themselves. This is particularly true in the case of sexual norms and values in many, if not all, religious groups in Europe, and, no doubt, elsewhere too. This is not a simple accident. There are complex psychological connections between sexuality, in the broadest sense, and the ritual use of the body. These connections will have to be examined later, but for the moment it is important to realise that because of this connection it is unlikely that people who do not share the same attitudes to sexual norms and ways of behaving, can share in the same ritual action in the same social situation. For example, when a group of Christians held a national 'Festival of Light' in Britain in September 1971, there was a counter demonstration organised at the same time by the various 'underground' groups. The point here is that given the attitudes to sexuality of the self-appointed groups of Christian moralists, anyone who thinks differently on this crucial area of sexuality cannot find it easy to join in ritual actions with them, but set up counter 'ritual' demonstrations.[7]

The most basic element in anyone's life is their body; its growth to maturity, especially sexual maturity, its state of health or ill-health, its wearing out, and finally its death and disappearance as a living organism. In all human societies, there is a large amount of ritual surrounding this natural cycle. Much of this ritual can put people in contact with the basic life process, and give them confidence to trust the body. However, it is also the case that cultural beliefs and values can so overlay this, that rituals come to put people out of contact with this natural process. Much of Western society's development in the area of ritual has done just this by concentrating on the supernatural realm, to the detriment, or even exclusion, of the natural. Many Christian thinkers have never seen this approach as authentically Christian, for it denies the point of the Incarnation, that the material world and man, biologically evolved man, is God-infused.[8] The influence of Manichean dualism has been so strong, however, that this view has been lost in popular thought in so-called Christian societies. Manichean dualism sees the material world and the body as evil, even created by the Devil, the spiritual alone is good and Godly. At the popular level, as distinct from some of the religious intellectuals, this view has been one of the most influential in both Catholicism and most forms of Protestantism. It has been very destructive for the rituals of Western societies. Many groups, both social and economic classes, and age groups, have found themselves in tension with Christian attitudes over sexuality, and thus with Christian rituals. British society has therefore reached a point where the central belief system and associated ritual system is one which is only partially acceptable. This situation is really quite tragic. People still look to Christian rituals, especially the life-cycle rituals, and find ritual action which often contradicts their own basic feelings. Instead of rituals being therapeutic and healing, emotionally and bodily, they become sources of further confusion. Take for instance the phrase in the marriage service, when the man puts a ring on the fourth finger of the woman's left hand, 'With my body I thee worship'. This phrase is the voice of 'authentic' ritual, and should aid the lovers to enjoy their sexuality. Yet in English churches it sounds out of place to many of them—sexuality in a church? Oh dear no!

TECHNICAL THEORY OF RITUAL ACTION

A sociology of ritual action cross-cuts a number of substantive areas in the sociology of social institutions, for it deals in part with religion, with art, and with politics. It also has to deal with the family as a setting for some ritual action. Such a sociology is concerned to understand and explain what are here called *ritual occasions*. These are social situations defined by the people themselves as separate, 'special' set-apart occasions, set apart from the world of work and from recreational activities.[9] Ritual action is related to serious values, *la vie serieuse* as Durkheim called it. It is this starting point for the definition of ritual *action* which distinguishes the action approach from that of theorists who take a more behavioural approach, defining ritual in terms of behaviour, which to an observer appears to be often repeated in the same rigidly stereotyped manner.[10] With the 'action approach' there seems no reason why a ritual occasion should necessarily be repeated, unless it is a traditional ritual. Whereas on the 'behavioural approach', ritual is defined in terms of rigidity and repetition. Furthermore, only on an action approach does it seem possible to deal adequately with explaining change in ritual, and the development of novelty in ritual actions.

Other authors have used 'ritual' in different ways from that suggested. Max Gluckman would call the general category 'ceremony', reserving the term 'ritual' for ceremony with a specific reference to mystical motions.[11] This type will be called 'religious ritual' in this book. There is a reason for using the term 'ritual' as a general category, similar to 'ceremony' in Gluckman, and that is that if the sociologist wants to deal with aspects of the arts, especially the performing arts, in an action approach to ritual, then it seems less of an abuse to ordinary English usage to describe theatre, ballet, opera, cinema, etc., under the general category 'ritual' rather than 'ceremony'—this latter term suggesting something more like the State Opening of Parliament. More precisely, ritual suggests the use of the human body, or parts of it, to articulate and express meaning—structures, which is the crucial common element of action of the kind of interest here. Such bodily ritual may be related to symbolic objects such as images, pictures, statues, flags, buildings, memorials, altars, food, etc. It is worth pointing out that the act of attending the serious occasion is itself the basic ritual action, the act of going to be present at it bodily, 'in person'. Watching ritual on television is always a second best, and sometimes will not count as attendance in the group being considered, for example, Catholics are required to attend Mass; watching a television ritual will not do.

The category of ritual action is not well established within sociology. This is so in spite of 'ritual' being a major analytical concept within anthropology. The problem centres around the fact that modern industrial societies, which are usually studied by sociologists, not anthropologists, are much more differentiated than the simpler societies of anthropology. Religious ritual is thought to be on the decline, at least in terms of emotional salience for the urban populations of Western Europe. Thus ritual has been seen by sociologists as of minor interest and importance for scientific analysis and study. However, this ignores the point that what, in a *less* differentiated society, is 'ritual' is much broader as a phenomenon than what, in a *more* differentiated society, is called 'religious ritual'. There is every reason to include many, if not all, artistic performances and entertainments, even sport, along with religious rituals, life-cycle rituals, and civic–political rituals in the analysis of the category 'ritual' in an urban, industrial society. This usage quite deliberately blurs the distinction often made by social scientists between religious rituals, which are said to be oriented to supernatural entities, and other types not so oriented.[12] It seems better to conceptualise religious beliefs as on a continuum, which has supernatural beliefs at one end, and scientific cosmological systems at the other. In between lie what Talcott Parsons has called 'conceptions of ultimate reality',[13] held by many people in a very non-articulated form. Also, by distinguishing religious ritual in terms of an element of the beliefs involved, the usual approach becomes too focused on intellectual ideas, rather than people's actual experiences. Many people would say that they believe in something they might call God, but this may bear little relation to what a sociologist means by classifying such a statement as 'a belief in a supernatural entity'.

The category, then, of ritual action as used here will include religious ritual, but also other types of ritual. Talcott Parsons' category of 'expressive symbolism' in *The Social System*[14] cross-cuts institutional areas, such as the family, religion, the arts, political institutions, in the same way. The category of ritual action is one type of expressive symbolism although Parsons does not himself make such a differentiation.

RATIONALITY AND RITUAL ACTION

The fact that ritual action still continues in modern industrial society is an important fact in itself, but is only a surprising one to those whose model of man underplays the importance of the non-rational elements in human beings. As was suggested in the first chapter, Weber did just that in his analysis of the development of rational action in modern Europe, for example, in his idea of the demystification, or demagification, of the world (*Entzauberung der Welt*). On the one hand Weber was right to pinpoint the growth and extent of rational action (formal rational, '*zweckrational*' action) in capitalist societies as being a crucial feature of these societies. On the other hand, Weber tended to assume that this process of the extension of rational action of this kind was possible to all areas of life without seeing that this may not be possible for human beings to tolerate.

Another writer Joachim Israel has discussed this aspect of Weber in his book on '*Alienation*' and shows, following Marcuse, that formal rationality in Weber is really based on a value assumption: 'Marcuse accuses Weber of having developed the ideological weapons for the defence of an irrational social system by concentrating on the descriptive aspects of formal rationality, rather than on a critical analysis, pointing out the consequences of "rationalisation"[15].

The notion of rationality, or reason, seems to carry an overtone of a cold, harsh, inhuman approach to the world of nature and men, as is shown in much of the literature of protest of the fifties and sixties.

One pursues a rational style of life, we say, if one's behaviour is characterised by dispassionate restraint, unfailing deliberateness, and an articulate logicality. Conversely, one is irrational if one's conduct forsakes dispassion in favour of an intense and overt emotionalism, deliberation in favour of impulsiveness, articulation and logic in favour of rhapsodic declamation or some manner of non-verbal expression.[16]

This refers very much to the emotional atmosphere surrounding 'science' in modern society, to the distortions through which people who do science in universities, and industry have to put themselves. But 'reason' has not always suggested this, nor has science. Lewis Feuer has shown in *The Scientific Intellectual* how the early scientists in Europe were 'libertarian hedonists', and not 'masochistic ascetics' of a Calvinistic type. From reading the first chapter of Feuer's study one sees that *for the individual* early science could fulfil all the requirements of ritual action; the linking of body and mind, the desires of the body and reason, and the working out of material from an unconscious base in the scientist's own self.

The scientific movement of the seventeenth century was not the by-product of an increase of repression or asceticism. It was the outcome of a liberation of energies; it derived from a lightening of the burden of guilt. With the growing awareness that happiness and joy are his aims, man could take frank pleasure in the world around him. Libidinal interests in external objects could develop unthwarted; the world was found fresh to live in—an unending stage for fresh experience.[17]

The critical problem with science has derived from the fact that it is not an easily shared experience. A large amount of time and energy has to go into learning the past work, and the abstract mathematical symbols used in scientific work. Few people are thus equipped to follow science anyway. When, as in the twentieth century, science is more a product of the work of teams, the result has been the mechanisation, routinisation, and specialisation of research. Similarly, in the education of scientists, the same processes have reduced the spontaneity, and the joy in doing science, in finding out, in exploring the world. Thus, we have reached a point where the group doing science cannot feel the connection between the work being done and each individual's own desires. Science becomes external, objective, to the individual, with little interest for him. Ritual action can involve members of groups, small and large, and does so by working with the whole of a person—his body, reason, unconscious needs and desires. It can appeal to symbols, actions, music, bodily movements, values and beliefs and ideas, and produce some momentary kind of unity.

The most crucial issue concerns the notion of rationality, for unless we have some clear view about man's rationality we can have no clear idea of what is to be explained in an analysis of ritual action. Susanne Langer developed an important distinction between discursive forms of symbolism and presentational forms, having first argued that man is a symbol producing being.

Language in the strict sense is essentially discursive; it has permanent units of meaning which are combinable into larger units; it has fixed equivalances which make definition and translation possible; its connotations are general so that it requires non-verbal acts like pointing, looking or emphatic voice inflections to assign specific denotations to its terms. In all these salient characters it differs from wordless symbolism, which is non-discursive and untranslatable, does not allow of definitions within its own system, and cannot directly convey generalisation.[18]

Langer's favourite example of a presentational form of symbolism is music; but ritual action is similar, where the symbolism is again non-discursive. So, for example, magic is not poor, applied science; it is a presentational form;[19] It is a ritual form of action. Susanne Langer is arguing for a theory of man, and of the mind, which includes logic, mathematics, language, but in addition—dreaming, art and ritual. The problem her work raises is how do the two areas connect? Are dreaming, ritual and art to be regarded as non-rational or not? The problem is most acute with regard to ritual, for dream symbolism, and symbolism in the arts, more clearly do belong to the area of human emotions, whether these be unconsious or not. Ritual, especially when it includes magical practices as well as religious ritual, does have components of emotional symbolism, but it also has beliefs and values associated with it in a way that art and dreaming do not. Thus, it is possible to pose the question of whether the beliefs are first, rational and second, true or false. It is important to distinguish the two issues. Whether a belief is rational is a separate issue from whether it is true or false. A belief is rational only in relation to some other belief. Martin Hollis argues

In agreeing with Miss Langer that ritual beliefs are to be identified by treating ritual utterances as acts of expressive, rather than presentational symbolism, I am taking rationality as a relation between beliefs. A ritual belief p is rational if and only if there is a belief q such that q supplies a reason for holding p and p does not entail the falsity of q.[20]

The anthropologist or sociologist can show the inner rationality of a group's beliefs and ritual actions, or their non-rationality, using basic notions of inference, contradiction, negation, which Hollis, among others, claims are universal to all notions of 'being rational' in any language and culture. He must make a separate judgement about the empirical truth or falsity of some of the beliefs.

Just because a belief is known to be false by the sociologist or anthropologist, or thought to be false, it does not follow that it is irrationally related to other beliefs. Indeed it may continue to be believed because it is rationally related to other specific beliefs in a belief system. The belief in purgatory, and the associated rituals, such as paying for masses for the soul of a dead person, as used to happen in mediaeval Catholic Christianity, is an example. The positing of a state of purgatory solved many problems about what happened to people who died having sinned a little, but not enough to be condemned to hell for ever by an all-loving God. This was a fairly rational way to solve the problem of theodicy in Christianity. Many sociologists may not believe there is such a state as purgatory, but they ought to be careful to distinguish that judgement from the one which would then see the belief as irrational, and therefore needing an explanation in terms of concepts about the irrational, such as the unconscious.

There is, however, another sense of rational ritual action, distinct from the one concerning the relation of beliefs to ritual. This second type has to do with the type of emotions and feelings associated with the ritual. It has been common for people influenced by psycho-analytic perspectives to see all ritual action as irrational, in the sense that it is motivated by unconscious emotions out of ego control, i.e. out of rational control. Ritual has been seen as equivalent to the obsessional actions of neurotics. However, others have maintained a distinction between rational and irrational rituals. For example, Erich Fromm does so in *Psycho-Analysis and Religion*. Fromm is clear that ritual is *socio-cultural* action, as can be seen in his definition of ritual as 'shared action expressive of common strivings rooted in common values'.

The rational differs from the irrational ritual primarily in its function; it does not ward off repressed impulses but expresses strivings which are recognised as valuable by the individual. Consequently it does not have the obsessional-compulsive quality so characteristic of the irrational ritual . . .[21]

This type of distinction makes it possible to distinguish social ritual from ritual of individuals with particular obsessions. It is the former which are of interest to the sociologist, and the latter to the psychiatrist and psycho-therapist.

Some rituals can be performed by groups which have a relatively coherent set of reasons for performing them, and the ritual actions are carried out free from anxiety and fears associated with neurotics' obsessional acts. Conversely it follows that some ritual actions could be performed by people who have no set of coherent reasons, potentially, if not actually, available to them. Here the type of explanation offered by psycho-analysis might be more appropriate. The crucial thing so far, however, is that the sociologist, anthropologist, or psycho-analyst must make a judgement about the degree of rationality involved in a particular group's ritual actions *before* he can know what type of explanation of the ritual is necessary. There is no possibility of the social scientist himself being able to decide this without a detailed familiarity with the action, and set of actions, in question. Anthropologists obtain this by living in the group they wish to study for long periods of time, and then trying to show the reasons the people themselves believe they have for their ritual actions, and they should also come to some kind of assessment of the coherence of these beliefs in relation to the actions. This is not the same as coming to a judgement about the truth or falsity of the beliefs, in the first instance. The psycho-analyst will gain detailed information about the meaning of ritual acts performed by his patients after hours of work with them. On the basis of such detailed information a judgement can be made about the rationality, or otherwise, of an individual's own rituals. No simple blanket judgements are possible in these matters. So it cannot be simply asserted whether a given person's religious acts are or are not to any degree rational or reasonable. (Incidentally, this assumes that the psycho-analyst is one who operates with this distinction; if his belief system does not allow for rationally held beliefs about ritual action then he will analyse all ritual as irrational.) In the case of sociology there are fewer examples of detailed studies of a group's beliefs, values and rituals, which include assessments of the reasonableness of the relations between these in any explicit way. Bryan Wilson's *Sects and Society* is perhaps an exception to this, as is Thomas O'Dea's *The Mormons*.[22] It is interesting that these are studies of sectarian movements in modern, urban societies, and not the central churches and denominations of Christianity. It may be that many sociologists who have studied the main churches assume that they are reasonable groups, i.e. have some coherent reasons for their rituals. However, it seems unlikely that this is true of all the many and varied rituals of all the major denominations of Christianity. For it is worth pointing out that mainstream Christianity includes exorcism, faith-healing of many varieties, speaking with tongues, baptism, communion, regular worship in the form of singing and praying, listening to the sacred scriptures being read, and hearing preachers of various types preaching. It seems much more likely that sociologists have not in fact made many considered judgements about the reasonableness of the various types of ritual action within mainstream Christianity, but rather they have taken a number of routes to avoid such detailed judgements.

One route is to shelter behind the idea that social scientists do not and should not make 'value-judgements' about politics or religion. All perspectives about living are as reasonable as the next, to this type of sociologist. To explain Fascism, Nazism, racism, Stalinism, and their contemporary equivalents is not distinct from explaining democratic socialism, or modern liberal capitalism. But if some of these ideologies are more rational than others, this will require preliminary work to be done to show this, and then the type of explanation required for a more rational, and less rational, ideology, will be different. This type of issue is rarely faced systematically in sociology.

Another route to avoid judgements about rationality is to assume that one's own set of assumptions as a sociologist are the most rational available to modern man and to analyse all others as belonging to a less rational category. In one sense this is inevitable. The author can do nothing else but see his own views as the best he can arrive at at a given point in time. However, what is required is some degree of argument for the ideas which are held to be more reasonable than another set, whereas what usually happens is that the assumptions are left implicit in the type of analysis the sociologist chooses to do. David Martin has sketched an outline of how this has happened in relation to the issue of secularisation, although his own pre-suppositions are left implicit.[23]

There is a worrying strand in much of the work produced by scholars who seem over-anxious to stress rationality. They seem to reassert the claims of the ego, of logic and the rational mind, over those of the body, its desires, feelings and pleasures. It does this in the way Alexander Lowen suggests, in *The Betrayal of the Body*, by allowing the ego to be supreme and dominate, rather than working with and for, the body [24]. Rationality alone puts all the stress on the mind, and on the use of words to find meaning in life. What gets left out are feelings, and yet it is these which often make experience meaningful for people. Words can articulate this when they reflect feelings, otherwise they are cold and barren. The rationalist seeks to eradicate all such overtones of what are to him 'mere feelings'.

Ritual action should not be seen as necessarily irrational, or non-rational. *Irrational action* is action to which certain rational criteria could be applied, and which fails to meet these criteria. Some magical action may be of this kind; this type could be replaced by technological action if and when rational criteria were applied. *Non-rational action* is action which cannot be assessed by any rational criteria because they are inapplicable, for example, the feelings involved in loving a person. Ritual action is best seen as to some extent rational, and also non-rational at times.[25] The sense in which ritual can be rational needs to be made explicit. It is that reasons can be given for engaging in the ritual actions which are coherent in that they connect with one another to form a reasoned argument.

The central point is to avoid seeing ritual always as irrational. Rationality is a set of tools for deciding on the validity of the connections between reasons offered for conclusions; it cannot guarantee any particular ontology, nor any particular value system. As far as we can see there are a number of such possible ontologies and value systems each of which may be internally rational, but it is not necessarily possible to chose between them on rational criteria alone.[26]

ANTHROPOLOGY AND RITUAL

The analysis of ritual in this book turns on the distinctions made between four types of ritual action in industrial society: religious, civic, life-cycle and aesthetic rituals. Basically they are analytical types, and thus any concrete ritual may well have more than one of the analytical components in it. The usefulness of the analytical distinction lies in making it possible to identify the elements of actual ritual action, and to make the richness of some ritual action more comprehensible. Without some such analytical types, it is very difficult to begin to write about ritual action at all. The merits of analytical distinctions lie in their usefulness to people in gaining more understanding of ritual actions; they are not meant to be discoveries of basic unchangeable, absolute categories of of ritual experience. Other ways of dividing up ritual may be much more useful for purposes other than those of this particular analysis.

These purposes are related to issues arising out of the attempt to gain some understanding of ritual action in industrial society. The work done by many anthropologists, and some psychologists, is very valuable for starting such an attempt, but it is limited in many respects. The most important of these is related to the typical conception of a society which operates in anthropological writing on rituals. This conception is one which stresses the unity of a society and culture, and the way a society of this kind persists over time and maintains itself.[27] This model of society may well be useful, and even to some extent true, in relation to many of the societies which have been studied by anthropologists, but it is a highly disputed one when applied to industrial societies, especially those with capitalist economies. The typologies of ritual developed by anthropologists often reflect this basic assumption about the unity of a social system, and cannot be taken over directly into a sociology of industrial societies which contain social conflicts, and lack harmonious integration—partly because they are much, much larger than the societies typically studied by anthropologists. There is a crucial sense in which ritual action in modern industrial societies is important for sociologists' model of these societies, for it is very much around ritual action that one might expect to see the unified aspects of the culture being maintained.[28] On the other hand, if there are major groups in the society who do not find that the main rituals of the nation resonate with them, then there is little point in working with the 'integrationist' model of society. It would seem more useful to use one which bears on the real meaning of the rituals to the people concerned, and to their perceptions of the society.

Within sociology itself, as it has developed in this century, the issue of whether to adopt a system model, or a conflict model, of society has been dominant in the theoretical discussion of sociologists.[29] The place of rituals in a social group, or society, is important in this debate; for example, if one looks at Durkheim he makes ritual a central part of his analysis of the way societies cohere over time.

D

THE RELATION OF THE PROBLEM OF MEANING
AND RITUAL ACTION

The problem of meaning has been discussed in fairly intellectual-istic terms by many sociologists since Max Weber, and primacy has been given to cognitive beliefs as components of solutions to the meaning problem. Yet for most people in human societies, the problem arises at certain points in their lives—life-crisis points—and it is then that the problem of meaning is raised in an acute emotional form. It is perhaps important to see that life crises are not all negative; some of the most joyful and positive experiences could raise a problem of meaning for some people. This would be similar to what Weber meant when speaking of a 'theodicy of good fortune'.[30] However, a more satisfactory way of seeing the issues is to relate the joy and sorrow, the good and evil, together. It is this which raises the emotional problem of theodicy: how are the two aspects of living to be kept in relationship to one another. For some individuals and groups, the main problem will be how to avoid being overwhelmed by evil and unhappiness; for others, how to accept joy in their own lives amidst suffering elsewhere. For example, the Russian anarchist Prince Kropotkin:

> What right had I to these higher joys when all around me was nothing but misery and struggle for a mouldy piece of bread; when whatsoever I should spend to enable me to live in that world of higher emotions must needs be taken from the very mouths of those who grew the wheat and had not bread enough for their children?[31]

These issues are posed for most people at the level of feelings, rather than as intellectual problems. Religious virtuosi, and specialists, do formulate such problems as rational ones, re-quiring intellectual work to be done on them. But in the main world religions, including Christianity, such ways of raising the questions about good and evil remain for the specialists, ordinary laity's interest in the intellectual formulations is again in their relation to feelings.

It is ritual action which can enable people to feel their way to a satisfactory handling of these issues, especially at points of life-crisis. Such a concentration on feelings may be seen as irrational by intellectuals, both scholars and theologians in the religious tradition itself, and by secular intellectuals analysing the action. However, such is not the view taken here; feelings are not simply dismissable as irrational. It is as has been shown earlier only on some views of 'reason' that feelings are seen as irreconcilable with the rational intellect. It is possible to see such a split notion of man as itself unreasonable; the more reasonable position is one which sees man as a whole being, with a mind which serves and guides feelings. Reason, which embraces the intellect and feelings, as in important works of art and the work of some scientists, is one of mankind's great blessings. The use of reason divorced from feelings—this may eventually exterminate us.[32] Ritual action which can articulate for people ways of finding resolutions to the problem of meaning and evil, which may be permanent, long-term, or temporary solutions, is a highly valuable possession of human cultures.

Our society does possess large numbers of such ritual actions; it is thus not as secular, nor thoroughly technological, as some people suggest. On the whole we are not sensitised to notice or see this. One advantage of Talcott Parsons' model of social systems built up of four sub-systems is to show that all societies must provide some way of dealing with such problems—what he terms 'pattern maintenance' and 'tension management'.[33] The problem with this language is that it tends to suggest that such 'tension-management' action is primarily equipping actors to go back and produce in the 'real' world of the economic system. However, his more general category of 'consummatory' action (which also includes integration) is a better term, for it suggests the other possibility that men may see this as an end in itself, not only as a means of refreshing themselves to go back to work. Both possibilities are needed: sections of a society, if not the whole society, may see either production and work as the end, or consummatory activities as the end, and work as the means. Rituals, in the broad sense used here, are then capable of being developed for some 'consummatory' activities: religion and art being the two major examples of ritual action which some people will regard as ends in themselves, not just means to ends, such as health, wealth, or success—but what life is for.

TYPOLOGIES OF RITUAL

The category of ritual action as used here includes not just religious ritual, but also aesthetic ritual, especially the performing arts, rituals of the life cycle and life crises, and civic and political ritual. In highly industrial societies each of these is relatively independent of the other; in less industrial societies, such as ancient Greece as the ideal-typical example, they were seen as a unified whole.[34]

The most recent sophisticated analysis of ritual and the literature on ritual has been made by Anthony Wallace. He uses five categories for types of ritual: ritual as technology; ritual as therapy and anti-therapy; ritual as social control; ritual as salvation; ritual as revitalisation. All of these are special cases of what he calls 'transformations of state' of either human beings or the natural world.[35] This particular focus is meant to reflect what people say they are doing in their rituals: 'What do the performers of religious ritual say they are trying to do?'[36] This is distinct from asking about the validity of religious beliefs, the essence of the religious experience, the meaning of religious symbols, the functions of religion, and the efficacy of ritual itself. There is something about this approach which leaves one wondering what questions can be asked by a sociologist or anthropologist; it seems to mean all that can be done is to report what people say they are doing. But the conditions under which they say this are not specified—is it in an interview with a social scientist, or in conversation in a family when trying to persuade a child to perform a ritual? Whatever the circumstances, Wallace does not in fact quote anybody's actual words, except those of social scientists, but he constructs his own categories. This is fine, but it is not what he says he is going to do.

Wallace seems to want to treat what Weber called subjective meaning to the actor seriously, and yet thinks that the only technique available for doing this is to take what people say they are doing in a fairly literal and superficial way as being this subjective meaning. This is, however, too easy. Even very verbal, literate, people, such as poets, find some experiences difficult, if not impossible, to put into words. The obvious, but important, example is the experience of listening to music. What is expressed in musical notes cannot be expressed in words, which is why it is worth listening intently to music. So what can the sociologist do? It has been suggested here that some help can be derived from phenomenologists' work, deriving from Husserl.[37] Such a philosophy is quite distinct as a basis for sociology from that of empiricism, positivism, or pragmatism, and thus needs discussion in philosophical terms, which cannot be done here. However, it is important to point out that most of the notions of what counts as social reality, and therefore as evidence in social science, derives from one or other of the philosophical alternatives to phenomenology, and are strictly inapplicable to the approach adopted here, unless they are found, when examined, to be usable within a phenomenological framework.

Wallace's valuable work, therefore, must be seen as built on certain pragmatist philosophical notions, and at times on empiricist and positivist notions, which lead him to ignore what he might see as unscientific modes of approach to human experience, in this case that of phenomenology and allied methods of working. His typology of rituals is heavily influenced by his philosophical assumptions, and, therefore, puts stress on the uses, or functions, of ritual. Alternatively, the typology of ritual developed here rests more on *the nature of the experience* in the different types of ritual. It still remains the case that rituals are used by groups for a variety of purposes, and that these purposes could themselves be categorised, but this is not the same as a set of categories for types of ritual *per se*.

The types used here reflect relatively discrete areas of ritual action, which are quite well differentiated in modern industrial society, but there are some empirical cases of rituals where a number of the types of ritual, as developed here, are fused. The social structures which have developed reflect the different types of experience of the four types of ritual. Churches are becoming centred around the numinous, the ritual action of worshipping as a Christian community, and even the Church of

England may soon have reached the position of being dis-established, and thus of loosening its ties with the nation state and its civic rituals.[38] Theatres, dance halls, opera houses, are specialised for providing aesthetic experiences, which are 'ritual' action as defined here. This is especially true of the 'performing arts'. Cinema, and parts of television, are also involved in this process of providing aesthetic ritual. (Cinema and television can also be involved in transmitting a civic ritual, or a religious one.)

Civic ritual is provided by the State, local government, the armed forces and Buckingham Palace. All organisations have some degree of ritual—often around changes in role, such as entry and leaving, or being promoted. Families too may provide rituals of a civic kind, although they are mainly concerned with natural-cycle rituals. Natural-cycle rituals are provided by the established Church still, although this raises problems for the clergy about the meaning of baptism and marriage for non-Christians. The State provides these too, especially marriage and funerals, which become more differentiated from religious ritual as such. Medicine is involved in providing some kind of ritual action for those who are sick.

Wallace also distinguishes between calendrical and non-calendrical rituals: 'Calendrical rituals occur on a regular schedule, and the occasion for their performance is always an event in some natural cycle—day and night, the waxing and waning of the moon, the seasons, eclipses, positions of the planets and stars'.[39] The distinction is useful as a minor distinction within a broader framework, but the category of non-calendrical rituals is too large as it stands for use here. Life-cycle rituals are the major category of natural-cycle rituals to be used here, and this will include not just birth, marriage and death, but also health and sickness as a cycle involving the use of ritual action.

RITUAL AND SOCIAL GROUPS

Audiences and Congregations

A theatre or cinema audience is a relatively ephemeral entity. Usually the members of an audience are unknown to one another;

or rather the various peer groups or families which make it up are unknown to one another, and heterogeneous. This is most true of cinema audiences, less true of some theatre audiences in a provincial town, or specialist theatres such as Covent Garden, where there are often many interconnections between some of the groups. A congregation on the other hand is defined, typologically here as a group consisting of peer groups and families who often do know one another because they meet fairly regularly, nearly every week at the church service.[40] It is this regularity of attendance which often means audiences at opera or ballet, small theatres, or cinema clubs, come to know one another more than is typical among theatre audiences. It is important to note, however, that in the case of the congregation the interaction among people in the congregation is increasingly positively sanctioned, and legitimated by the value system of Christianity. There is a negative value attached to the activity of using a church service as something to be watched, as an audience watches a film, a play, or an opera. A member of a congregation should participate by saying 'Amen' periodically, praying either inwardly or in spoken words, by singing the hymns and psalms, and by moving together with the rest of the congregation in standing, sitting, kneeling, taking communion, and giving in money to the collection. A member of an audience can be entirely passive outwardly once he or she has purchased the ticket: hence many people are highly disturbed by the thought of audience participation, especially if they have no option about being involved. Clearly a member of an audience cannot be entirely uninvolved, he or she must appear to be inwardly alert to the action, and to laugh and applaud in the correct places. It is deviant to fall asleep, even in cinemas. Crucially, though, the theatre has no value system which exhorts audiences to get to know one another over a period of time, in the way that this is sanctioned in a congregation.

There are many similarities between audiences and congregations, but it is important to have them distinct to begin with as types of social groups. For the study of ritual in industrial society, as distinct from the rural, agricultural, less complex, smaller societies studied by anthropologists, the boundaries of the group are much more difficult to draw. The functions of ritual in industrial society are different from those in less complex, less differentiated societies. In the latter they express 'collective conscience' and are the basis of what Durkheim termed 'mechanical solidarity'. In industrial society, the division of labour gives society the degree of organic solidarity which it possesses. These Durkheimian types are analytically useful; some ritual action though still operates in subcultures and substructures in a way analogous to those in simpler societies. But on the whole, at the level of the total society this is rarely the case. Rituals can be used in modern society for coming to know ourselves as individuals, as our own centre of action. 'The individual feels himself less *acted upon*; he becomes more a source of spontaneous activity . . .'

> As all the other beliefs and all the other practices take on a character less and less religious, the individual becomes the object of a sort of religion. We erect a cult on behalf of personal dignity, which, as every strong cult, already has its superstitions. It is thus, if one wishes, a common cult, but it is only possible by the ruin of all the others, and, consequently, cannot produce the same effects as this multitude of extinguished beliefs. There is no compensation for that. Moreover, if it is common in so far as the community partakes of it, it is individual in its object . . . It is still from society that it takes all its force, but it is not to society that it attaches us; it is to ourselves. (E. Durkheim.[41])

Communities

One of the crucial features of some rituals is the expression of community and community support in those areas of industrial society where such community identity exists. Communities are not formed merely by the fact that people live in close geographical proximity, although this assumption can be found in sociological literature. For example, Schnore defines community

> as the localised population which is interdependent on a daily basis, and which carries on a highly generalised series of

activities in and through a set of institutions which provides on a day-to-day basis the full range of goods and services necessary for its continuity as a social and economic entity.[42]

This contrasts with other ways sociologists have looked at community, such as Ferdinand Tonnies in *Gemeinschaft und Gesellschaft*. The theory of *Gesellschaft* 'deals with the artificial construction of an aggregate of human beings which superficially resembles the *Gemeinschaft* in so far as the individuals live and dwell together peacefully. However, in *Gemeinschaft* they remain essentially united in spite of all separating factors, whereas in *Gesellschaft*, they are essentially separated in spite of all uniting factors.'[43] *Gesellschaft* comes to develop more fully in modern industrial societies, although some social relationships were of this type under feudalism in Europe, and in the modern period there are some elements of *Gemeinschaft*, even in the modern corporation. Nevertheless, there is an important difference between the two types of social relationships. For Schnore, it is open to investigation how far any given social unit he defines as a community has 'we-feeling', or, one might add, relationships of a *Gemeinschaft* type. It seems useful to keep both terms in sociology, one to refer to a type of social unit, smaller than a whole nation-state, larger than an organisation, or a small group, such as the family; the other to refer to a special type of social relationship.[44] *Gemeinschaft* relationships are based on deep levels of emotion and feeling, rather than the rational calculation of *Gesellschaft*; they involve the whole of existence, rather than a segment of it.[45] Often, described in this way, even in abstract sociology, there is the tendency to regard *Gemeinschaft* relationships as more desirable and better than those of *Gesellschaft*. (For instance, many readers of Martin Buber find his I-Thou relationship of this desirable type.)[46] But this is to overlook the very important achievements of societies which have large amounts of *Gesellschaft* relations, even are typified by them—the breaking-away from traditionalism, from rigid codes of morality and convention. It is important to realise that no matter what we of the last part of the twentieth century think of modern societies' so-called 'loss of community', the people who moved away from feudalistic *Gemeinschaft* society did so thinking they were making a step towards human freedom.[47]

Rituals in a *Gemeinschaft* type of society had, and still have, a depth of communal feeling which is so often felt to be lacking in some modern rituals carried out in *Gesellschaft* conditions. For example, one might think of the difference in experiential terms between seeing a film, or a play involving the enactment of a ritual, and actually participating in it oneself, not as an actor but in social reality. The modern member of an audience experiences feelings in an individualised form, in a very internal mode, with almost no body movement. The member of a *Gemeinschaft* group participating in a ritual is involved as a member of the group, who has very little awareness of himself as an isolatable individual. People who have been educated out of their local areas with some degree of '*Gemeinschaft*' about them, often experience this separateness when they return after some years to attend perhaps a funeral, or other ritual, in the old setting. Unless many others have also moved away, the individual who has done so will feel a peculiar sense of estrangement from the rest of the group which is collectively involved. For example, the young son in the play *The Contractor* by David Storey is in this position at the wedding of his sister and the preparations for it.

Perhaps the central problem in ritual occasions in industrial society revolves around the group in which it takes place, for this will affect the type of experience members can have. Here the work of social psychiatrists is of great value for understanding ritual, the meaning and quality of the experiences people have.[48] For example, the number of times a group has met will affect the experience. If it is an audience, the chances are that the particular group is a unique mix of individuals and groups. A congregation is likely to have met over a longer period of time, at least its core members are. In many family rituals the members will often be very well known to one another; in experimental theatre a group of actors and/or the participating audience may have met over a number of months or even years. (Note here *The Rite*, a film by Bergmann, where a small group of three have worked together for years in creating experimental theatre, including ritual theatre.[49])

A ritual within a hippy commune will have different dimensions again for the participants, as a result of the community having lived and shared life together for a long period of time.

There are two dimensions involved in ritual occasions. There is the group itself who participate in some way in the ritual, and here participation importantly includes the appreciative audience; and there is the rituals' symbolic system. There are the following dimensions to the group:

(*a*) The nature of the social relationships of the members: kin, work colleagues, peers, age-grades, strangers.

(*b*) The length of time members have known one another, ranging from never before, at previous meetings of the groups, months, years, or whole life-cycles to the present.

(*c*) The range of other activities the members are involved in. (This is what Amitai Etzioni has termed 'Scope'.[50])

Chapter Three

Ritual: Civic and Religious

It is necessary first of all to distinguish two major forms of ritual activity when trying to understand the highly differentiated societies of Europe and America. There is on the one hand what will be termed 'civic ritual', and on the other 'religious ritual'.[1] All ritual action is distinguished from other types of action on the basis of the action being oriented to sacred or charismatic objects (material things, persons, or animals), that is objects which are set apart from the profane world, the everyday world of routine and utilitarian action. In order to avoid the specifically religious connotations of the term 'sacred' which Durkheim uses, the term 'charismatic' is preferable since it connotes both religious and civic charisma. In religious ritual the charismatic objects which people relate to are 'holy' or sacred, in R. Otto's sense of this term.[2] 'Holy' persons or things are culturally defined as being in contact with, or capable of evoking in others, the numinous dimension of human experience; in Christianity the cause of the numinous in human experience is held to be a transcendental God, who created and continues to create and sustain the material universe and everything in it. In civic ritual the charismatic objects related to are not connected with the holy sphere, even though they are set apart from the profane world. In a culture like that of England, which has preserved rituals in many areas now clearly differentiated from the Church, there are many examples of civic ritual of this type. Some of these rituals may historically have originated in connection with the Church, others may not, but this is not the issue here; the origins of the rituals are not relevant to an analytical distinction between types. Civic rituals can be found in groups of all kinds—the nation as a whole, a town, a city, a school, a university, army regiments, courts of law, political parties, and even industrial companies (giving someone a gold watch).

In order to explain the persistence of civic ritual in groups of this kind the functionalist notion of 'integration' would seem to have some value; the ritual occasion brings members together, and makes them aware of their membership of the group. Such ritual occasions also serve pattern maintenance functions, by reminding people of the basic values which the group rests upon, and renewing commitment to these values on the part of members. In many of these rituals, people are made aware of 'society', its laws and the obligations of its members, of something more powerful than themselves standing over and above them.

Durkheim's analysis of the rites of Australian aborigines led him to explain religion, and the idea of the sacred, by saying that the participants in the rites did experience a reality beyond them, on which they were dependent:

There is no doubt that a society has everything needed to arouse in men's minds simply by the influence it exerts over them, the sensation of the divine, for it is to its members what a God is to his faithful. For a God is first a being whom man imagines in certain respects as superior to himself, and on whom he believes he depends, whether we are speaking of personalities like Jacob, Zeus, or Jahweh, or of abstract forces like those which come into play in totemism. In either case, the believer feels that he is obliged to accept certain forms of behaviour imposed on him by the nature of the sacred principle with which he feels he is in communication. But Society also maintains in us the sensation of a perpetual dependence, because it has a nature peculiar to itself, different from our individual nature and pursues ends which are likewise peculiar to itself; but since it can attain them only through us, it imperiously demands our co-operation . . .

Society awakens in us the feeling of the divine. It is at the same time a commandment which imposes itself and a reality qualitatively superior to individuals which calls forth respect, devotion, adoration.[3]

Durkheim's analysis was developed in relation to a less differentiated society than modern England, and thus civic and religious ritual were undifferentiated empirically in the societies he was studying, and he did not fully distinguish between them. The failure to do so vitiates his explanation of 'the sacred', the Holy, as being an experience of 'society'. If this explanation is to be a testable theory, the term 'society' has to mean a particular social system of which the participants in the rite are members, which may be a tribe or clan, or a nation-state, or an organisation. In this case, especially in modern societies, it is clear what is being asserted—the rituals relate to the specific group of members, and their experiences of the situation could be established by interviews after they had taken part in a ritual occasion, to find out the meaning the occasion had for them. The point is that there is a great difference between the experience of someone who has taken part in a 'civic ritual' and someone who has taken part in a religious one. The former does not imply any necessary connection with the 'Holy' in the way the latter does, and it is not legitimate for the sociologist to simply treat the two experiences as identical, as a strict Durkheimian approach would seem to entail. The distinction is analytical; empirically some rituals will be a mixture of the two, e.g. the Coronation service; the funeral of a national figure such as Winston Churchill; Remembrance Day activities; or a speech day with hymns and prayers, or morning assembly in schools.

The key test for this distinction comes in relation to the churches themselves. When members of a parish church meet for worship, part of the ritual action involves, no doubt, creating a consciousness of membership of the group, i.e. the church, and renewing commitment to its norms and values. This may be achieved by the singing of hymns by all the congregation, all taking part in the communion (a point which is being stressed more and more in some churches), and being taught the values of the church in sermons. Analytically this is partly 'civic ritual' even though it takes place in a church. Is there, then, anything that can be properly called 'religious ritual'?

Many sophisticated believers would certainly reply 'Yes,

there is something else'. For example, Evelyn Underhill,[4] in discussing worship, says worship is adoration and praise: 'Holy, Holy, Holy, Lord God of Hosts. Heaven and *earth* are full of Thy Glory . . .' (from the Church of England Eucharist). There is an experience here which can be distinguished from that of 'collective effervescence'[5] which could occur when a congregation in a church were singing a hymn with a particularly 'stirring' tune. There is, however, nothing that can be said if a reductionist wants to reinterpret such numinous, holy, experiences as *really* experiences of society, and not of the Holy, something other, transcendent to mankind and his society. But this is strictly a philosophical and theological problem. Sociology of religion can for its own purposes 'bracket off' the ontological issues of the nature of the reality which believers experience—the main methodological point is that the experiences which worshippers have of a Reality beyond themselves must be treated as a basic datum; this is the meaning which they give to their activities, and to understand religious ritual this subjective meaning must be treated as fundamental to the action. It is not necessary to find sociological, or psychological, reasons to *explain* the basis of the experiences unless one is engaged in constructing a naturalistic account of the universe—a philosophical activity, which requires the built-in critique and scepticism of professional philosophy if it is to be indulged in at all meaningfully. The Durkheimian and Freudian accounts of religion are best seen as contributions to our understanding of *distorted* forms of religion. These may, empirically, be the most common forms of religious experience, nevertheless they are best treated theoretically as deviant types of experience, retaining the possibility of a purer type of religious experience, of 'true' worship as this would be understood by the members of a highly developed religion. These deviant types of religious experience are to be understood in the light of the concept of the ideal of religious worship as developed by a particular religious group. Only in the light of such a concept of 'true' worship can deviant forms be seen in a proper pespective. This point does not imply that the sociologist, *qua* sociologist, is committed to holding that these experiences are revealing of God, or gods, or do *really* put men in contact with God, or a supernatural realm; only that worshippers think and believe this to be the case.

The comparison between the two types of ritual can be made on the basis of three variables: the nature of the symbolism involved, the nature and degree of involvement on the part of the participants which is expected by the culture, and the culturally defined implications for other areas of life of participation in the ritual.

(i) *The Nature of the Symbolism*

Symbols in religious ritual have a reference to the Holy, those of civic ritual to the group and the secular world. The symbols may be special clothes worn only on ritual occasions, or material objects, or actions, or words, such as 'Hallelujah'.

The flag of a nation-state, for instance, is *used* as a symbol for a secular social group. An ikon in Orthodoxy is *used* as a symbol for, or even an instance of, the transfiguration of the material, natural, world by the supernatural, mystical world. (Unlike a painting in West European art of the last few centuries.) The meaning of a symbol is its use in concrete social situations. Some symbols can become 'meaningless' in the course of time.[6]

Talcott Parsons comes near to introducing a distinction similar to the one being made here:

> The religious type of expression of group solidarity is to be distinguished from collective solidarity symbolism which is evaluative in emphasis, but not religious in that there is no reference to legitimation in terms of a supernatural order. Examples would be patriotic observance, such as that of the Fourth of July in this country [i.e. USA] or the ceremonial of a university Commencement.[7]

The latter is what is being called here 'civic ritual', but the first type Parsons has, where there is a reference to the supernatural order, is an example, not of 'religious ritual' as used in this book, but of a mixed empirical type where both analytical elements are present. Parsons does not define religious expressive symbolism in a way that is compatible with the notion of

Photograph by Anthony Crickmay

1   London Contemporary Dance Theatre—*The Troubadors*. Dancer—
William Louther.

2   The coronation of Elizabeth II in June 1953.

3   The Ikon of Kursk in London, 1965. Religious ritual.

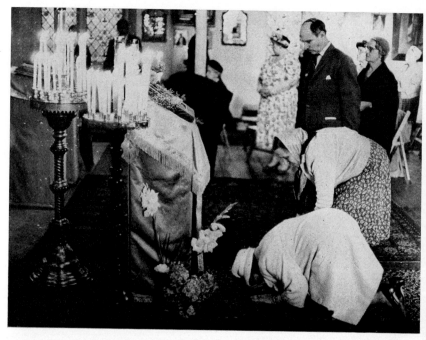

religious ritual developed here, for he remains over-influenced by the Durkheimian approach:

> We may . . . have religious symbolism expressive of the solidarity of the main institutionalised collectivities. We also have religious symbolism which serves as an institutionalised channel for the adjustment of emotional strains in the discrepancy areas.
>
> *The first was what Durkheim regarded as the core type of religious ritual, the symbolic expression of the solidarity of the group.* The second was the type especially emphasised by Malinowski, the type case being the funeral ceremonial.[8]

(ii) *The Nature of the Involvement of Participants*

Participants in religious ritual are expected to be highly involved in the meaning of the ritual; it is not an empty form which should be performed with no inner, subjective awareness. In civic ritual neither the principal participants nor the onlookers need cultivate deep understanding of the inner meaning of the ritual actions and symbols involved. This does not mean to say that they will have no emotions, nor that the ritual will have no consequences for the group, such as raised morale, or higher degree of integration, but that the cultural expectations on participants are not as great in civic ritual as in religious, nor are the rituals supposed to be experienced as deeply meaningful. People are culturally allowed to *watch* a civic ritual but should *participate* in a religious ritual.

(iii) *Implications for Other Areas of Life*

The implications of a religious ritual, such as the liturgy of churches, are wide ranging in their impact on the rest of the participants' lives; worshippers are to carry over into their whole lives the attitudes of praise, thanksgiving, adoration for the Holy, and in Christianity they are to love God and their neighbours. Civic rituals carry very few implications for other areas of life. In Catholic sacraments for example, participants receive grace from God to help them with their spiritual growth and lives; this is not reducible to the same thing as the recognition

E

of the raising of group morale in an army by parades and other military ceremonial, for no one believes that military ceremonies confer anything to the participants in the way grace is believed to be conferred on those receiving the sacraments. (Magic does not confer grace either and has implications for specific areas of life only, not the whole of life.)

The distinction between what has been called here 'religious ritual' and 'civic ritual' is, therefore, fundamental to establishing a sociology of ritual on a sound methodological and theoretical footing. Without it sociologists will continue to try to find naturalistic essences of the nature of religion in the tradition of Durkheim, Marx and Freud. Alternatively, they may fail to see the key importance of ritual to religion, to overstress the importance of beliefs in their analysis, and to see ritual in religious institutions as no more than the 'trappings' of a traditional institution.

The usefulness of the distinction between religious and civic ritual will be demonstrated in an examination of the problems that have grown up in England, particularly within the Church of England and between that Church and its relations with the other major institutions in England. To take the second point first, the Church of England has been involved in providing civic ritual for many groups outside the Church itself, including, perhaps most importantly, the nation itself. A ceremony such as the Coronation is a unique instance of this, where the civic ritual is today more dominant than the religious, although the latter aspect is not entirely lacking. The church has provided and still provides civic ritual for the community in various forms—such as local Remembrance Day services, where the dead soldiers of two world wars are commemorated.

Within Christianity generally, and the Church of England in particular, there are differences over the understanding of ritual between Protestants and Catholics. This is increasingly less so among many of the professionals in the various Churches, but still the case among many of the laity, for whom the issue of ritual is still of great importance. The Church of England contains groups of both theological positions within it which makes it a very interesting organisation for studying cultural elements such as ritual, with organisational structure held relatively constant. Protestants tend to see religious ritual as defined here as of less importance than Catholics, and tend in their talk about it to see it as either magic (which is meant as a negative judgement about it) or as an artistic performance, or as civic ritual.

The Catholic movement within the Church of England has stressed the role of specifically 'religious ritual' in church life, rather than civic ritual, in either sense—where the group which is the 'object' of the ritual orientation is either the church congregation, or an external group such as the local community or the nation, or an organisation. The Anglican Catholics have stressed the values expressed in the psalmic phrase 'Worship the Lord in the beauty of Holiness', and have emphasised the value of ritual action oriented to symbols of the Holy in worship.[9] They have tended to oppose many of the 'civic rituals' the Church performs: many for instance have opposed, and still oppose, the Establishment of the Church for a complex of reasons, included among which is the fact that an established Church has to provide 'civic rituals' for the nation state. They have also opposed 'civic ritual' in the church itself, where the congregation is the key reference point, as expressed in large amounts of hymn singing and rousing preaching, for they have held that worship is not for uplifting the congregation, not for its moral improvement, nor aesthetic pleasure, but primarily for the worship of the Holy.[10]

The recent phenomenon of Ecumenical Services, involving all the major Christian Churches in England—the Roman Catholic, Russian and Greek Orthodox, Anglican, Methodist, Baptist, Congregationalist, Quaker, Salvation Army (finally accepted by the Churches as a denomination, not a sect!)—produces an interesting situation where an attempt is made to use 'civic ritual' techniques, e.g. rousing hymns, to create among the congregation a sense of 'oneness'. Such services are not conducive to arousing or expressing a sense of the numinous, because there is such a wide variety of styles of worship present. Only music seems able to evoke collective effervescence.

The particular religious group given special attention in this

book, the Anglican Catholics, have been chosen for their
relevance to an important discussion at the heart of modern
sociology, namely what Max Weber called '*Entzauberung der
Welt*', the desacralisation of the world, after the Protestant
Reformation in Europe and North America.[11] One of the
major aspects of this process was the change from a ritual religion
to an ethical one—puritanical Protestantism. The recent
changes in the Roman Catholic Church in Europe and North
America can be understood within this framework too; the
emphasis being laid more than previously on ethical obligations,
rather than ritualistic obligations. The growth of Anglo-
Catholicism within the Church of England during the nineteenth century, and continuing into the twentieth, is a major
deviant case from the main direction of change. It marked the
recovery of the sacred and numinous dimension in a Church
which had been reformed and desacralised for more than two
centuries since the Reformation. The Anglican Church from
1700 to 1850 could be seen as a relatively desacralised religious
organisation, with a stress on puritan ethical conduct at the
individual level, and its ritual more civic than religious. The
development and growth of the Oxford Movement, followed by
the growth of Ritualism, mark an attempt to recover the sacred
dimension in what was the most advanced nation economically,
politically, and militarily at the time.[12]

According to Mary Douglas's analysis, educated Roman
Catholics have moved from a ritual religion to an ethical one.
Anglo-Catholicism could be seen as the reverse of this: a move
from an ethical religion in Anglicanism to a ritual religion,
among the educated too.[13] Is the case of this shift from ethical
to ritual action a 'deviant' case in the sociology of religion? The
usual assumption is that as a religion develops, especially in
industrial society, ritual declines and a this-worldly orientation
would occur and a more ethical religion grow.

The central concern of 'religious ritual', as the term has been
defined, is with worship. The other types of ritual are primarily
concerned with different aspects of human experience. Sociologists have not often given this element of worship much importance in their analyses of religion, presumably because the

idea seems to imply a socially unimportant activity. This is quite apart from the crude positivism which many social scientists have held, which would lead them to ignore subjective meanings of any action, whether it is religious or not. Yet even among those who do not rule out subjective meanings there tends to be suspicion of the notion of worship as the core of religion.[14]

When political groups meet, they may perform certain rituals which approach being religious, at least in external appearances, such as in singing political songs or hymns together, but they are not engaged primarily in worship. The people themselves would say that there is a difference. A religious congregation, in all highly developed religions, and in both Catholic and Protestant Christian Churches, would say that it is meeting together to worship, not itself, which is to them idolatry, but a god or God. They may or may not experience worshipful emotions in such a setting, but they are there to worship in ways defined by their particular religious group or Church.

Sociologists, and other social scientists, tend to inevitably have an attitude towards worship as an activity, which is bound to affect the way they approach religion as a social and human phenomenon. Worship in a particular religion may be seen as the most important activity possible by a believer in that religion, and if a sociologist is a believer this will tend to predispose him or her to an acceptance of the worthwhileness of worship, perhaps in many religions, not just the one to which he or she adheres. To others, worship seems a waste of time, boring, uninteresting, a way people can cope with their neurotic needs, a form of alienation in a society which excludes them from decisions over their own lives, a form of collective madness, in short anything but a worthwhile and important human action. These attitudes of sociologists to worship will reflect their own socialisation, their own psychic development, and their own beliefs about cosmology.

As mentioned in Chapter Two, there are two other types of ritual which can be usefully distinguished from religious and civic rituals. There are aesthetic rituals, concerned with experiences of aesthetic enjoyment and appreciation of symbols and gesture in their own right, as beautiful things. Also there are rituals of the life-cycle, concerned with crises and changes in the body over a whole life-span. They are usually embedded in religious and civic rituals, but they are analytically distinguishable in that they have a specific reference to people's experience of their bodies. These are discussed in later chapters.

STATISTICS OF ATTENDANCE AT RITUALS

How far do statistics, which show how many people in a given period of time attend certain types of ritual, measure something of significance to sociology? They really tell very little. They say nothing about the meaning of the ritual to the people, so that it is not possible to say that all the figures from different groups at different periods are strictly comparable. For example, attendance at Bach's *St Matthew Passion* is not counted as an indicator of 'religious' ritual attendance in this society, and yet it may be quite a significant event for many in the audience, certainly comparable with the meaning of some religious rituals to others, or even the same people. Similarly, the Remembrance Day rituals are observed by large numbers of people, especially buying a poppy. Is this to be counted as a religious ritual action? On many definitions of religion it certainly should be, although it may also have elements of civic ritual about it, being the sort of action an Englishman should perform. There is something unpatriotic about ignoring Poppy Day, especially among the older generation.

Statistics also focus on those who actually carry out the rituals, but say nothing about those who do not attend church rituals. This would not matter if no conclusions were ever drawn from the figures, but this is, of course, not the case. Falls in church attendance figures are used to justify the conclusion that secularisation is taking place; this is particularly so among some clergy, not just among social scientists. This may be the best way of interpreting the figures from the point of view of the Churches, but not necessarily the best from the point of view of sociology of religion. Sociologists ask different questions, or should do, about the relation between the fact that some people attend churches and the effects, if any, on the rest of social life. The numbers attending are to some extent beside the point if the real purpose of sociology is to seek understanding of the part religion plays in the life of a society and culture.

Bryan Wilson is ambivalent about statistics in the introductory section of *Religion in Secular Society*, where he says: 'One should not assume as sociologists often do that a unit of behaviour is, because it can be reduced to a statistic, invariably a quantity of the same weight and social significance.'[15] Wilson wants to argue that both America and England are secular societies even though the statistics in America of high church attendances would suggest otherwise. He argues that this is not really a measure of the influence of religion in the United States in terms of the influence of religious institutions and thinking. Yet for England the statistics are used as some kind of evidence for secularisation:

> What can be claimed for religious statistics is necessarily limited. The ways in which men express their 'religiosity' may be changing, and church attendance and ritual may be felt by some quite religiously disposed people to be outworn patterns unadapted to the modern world. And yet, all these various considerations notwithstanding, the statistics do provide some evidence of significant religious change. They are some sort of index of secularisation, taking that word at its common-sense value.[16]

Other writers interpret the 'evidence' differently, for example, David Martin.

> Yet if we except some mild erosion of the more conventional rites of passage and the special difficulties of non-conformists, the position seems to have been almost stationary since the war. Let it be said quite simply that in the course of a year nearly one out of every two Britons will have entered a church, not for an event in the life cycle, or for a special personal or civic occasion, but for a service within the ordinary pattern of institutional religion.[17]

This seems to be evidence against the common-sense notion of secularisation. (Perhaps it should be added that this concept is not one common among non-intellectuals. Wilson's common sense is not shared by many.) Talcott Parsons interprets the evidence in America differently from Wilson—Parsons sees differentiation of the religious sphere from others in modern society and within religious systems themselves as not necessarily evidence for secularisation. 'Our time by and large, however, is not one of religious complacency but, particularly in the most sensitive groups in these matters, one of substantial anxiety and concern.'[18] And

> However deep the ambivalence about the morality of profit-making may go, there can be little doubt that the main outcome has been a shift in social conditions more in accord with the general pattern of Christian ethics than was mediaeval society, provided we grant that life in this world has a positive value in itself.[19]

Chapter Four

Religious Ritual in the Church of England

CHANGE IN RELIGIOUS RITUAL—LITURGICAL REFORM

'Liturgy' will be used here to refer to the whole complex of ritual actions in the narrower sense of specific acts, such as making the sign of the cross, together with readings from the sacred scriptures, singing hymns and psalms, prayers and sermons which make up acts of worship. During the 1960s the Church of England, along with other Churches, has been revising its liturgy. There are a number of experiments going on at present with these revised liturgies in various churches, where the vicar and church council have agreed to try them for a period of time. This period of change has been problematic for some members of the laity, for it makes it very clear that liturgies are man-made, they are not absolute for all time, nor God-given. It is particularly problematic for some of the Anglo-Catholic congregations who have previously looked to the Roman Catholic Church as the authority and standard in these matters and have found the Roman Church changing its liturgical forms; and rules. For example, catholics in the Church of England had always paid a great deal of attention to fasting before taking communion, but the Church of Rome relaxed its rules on this matter when it introduced evening mass, and requires those taking communion to fast for one hour only before communion. The traditional rule had been not to eat anything before taking communion on the *day* of communion, hence the early morning communion, or mass, in the Church of England.[1]

In the process of liturgical reform there is a stress on the importance of both 'religious ritual' and 'civic ritual' where the church congregation is the reference. For example, the stress on the value of a general communion of all at the Eucharist has the intended consequences of increasing awareness of the collectivity assembled together (civic ritual).

One of the unintended consequences of the reform is to focus attention on the impact the liturgy makes on the congregation. Its effects on them becomes a major criterion for judging changes. This will in turn entail more concentration on what has been termed here 'civic ritual' where the group becomes the major object of concern and symbolism is interpreted in relation to the group. 'Religious ritual' would be judged by the criterion of its relevance to the worship of the Holy; this may mean in practice examining whether a particular liturgy has been used by the Church in the past, and whether it has a capacity to evoke spiritual feeling of the Holy in those regarded as most competent to judge this in the Church at a particular period. There is an appeal to both traditional authority—the undivided Catholic Church of early Christianity—and to the charismatic authority of contemporary liturgical specialists.

The liturgical changes which have been made in the Roman Church and in the Anglican Churches have been concerned to reduce the element of 'natural religion'[2] and of 'mystery cult' in the services of the Church, and to introduce changes that symbolise and evoke the view of the Church as a 'sacred community', with a participating laity, instead of the reliance on the words and actions of the priest alone. Thus the westward-facing position for Mass emphasises and symbolises the priest as representative of the community of believers, in place of the mystery cultus figure far away at the altar, with his back to the congregation. The Kiss of Peace, which involves the priest taking the hands of fellow priests and servers around the altar, and the congretation doing the same action, stresses the brotherly love of the Christian community, and the value of 'Peace which passes all understanding'.

Having established that religious ritual is distinct from ritual in which the group is the focus of worship, it is necessary to look in more detail at how religious ritual is itself differenti-

ated, how it is produced and sustained, and what its effects are
on the participants. Here the work of Durkheim and his group,
especially H. Hubert and M. Mauss, is a useful starting point,
even though the fundamental assumption of Durkheim, that
religious ritual has the group as its focus always, has been
rejected. Durkheim's fundamental distinction between the
sacred and the profane is an important starting point. His
claim that such a distinction can be found in all religions may
not be entirely true of every human group studied by Western
anthropologists, but it is certainly very widespread empirically,
and has not disappeared in modern industrial society. Religion
is built fundamentally on this division between sacred and
profane things, places, times, people; they radically exclude
each other. Sacred things are set apart by interdictions, and
negative rites, from profane things.[3] Durkheim goes on to
distinguish religion from magic in terms of the nature of the
relation between those who use a magician, as relatively
isolated individuals seeking help on specific issues, and those in
the same religious group united into a Church, a single moral
community.[4]

There are difficulties in using Durkheim's distinction in the
way he formulated it in examining a Church such as the modern
Anglican Church, and even the Roman Catholic Church, in that
their new liturgies are not built on the basis of ideas which
make the same radical distinction which Durkheim suggests
between sacred and profane. Rather, the new liturgies rest on the
idea of bringing the common and the holy together. 'The marks
of the liturgy in future are likely to be informality, flexibility and
continuity with ordinary life-style, so that there is no forced
sense of stepping out of one world into another, no compulsory
cultural circumcision as one "enters church".'[5] Here there
are complex theological issues involved about the nature of
Christianity and its ultimate aims; suffice it to say that there has
always been a push towards making the common holy, sancti-
fying the secular, and breaking out of the rather rigid sacred–
profane dichotomy as formulated by Durkheim.

Organised religious groups in Christianity have nevertheless
had a tendency towards this separation of sacred and profane,

and the Church of England still had this in modern England. Anglicans, like other denominations, still dress in their 'best' clothing when they attend church, and the atmosphere in most Anglican churches is one of separation from the ordinary world, especially in those with stained glass windows and organs playing. The new ideas of liturgy are still ideas of the religious virtuosi, although some younger members of congregations often welcome change from the old style of 'sacred' services.

In order to understand more adequately what is happening today in religious ritual it is necessary to develop the Durkheimian distinction more fully, and in some respects rather differently. Thomas O'Dea distinguishes eight characteristics of Durkheim's notion of the sacred: it has superior seriousness and dignity when compared with the profane; it involves the recognition of a power or force behind nature and cosmos, attractive and repugnant, helpful and dangerous to me; it is non-utilitarian, non-empirical and does not involve knowledge, but rests on feelings and experiences of a non-sensory kind; it gives support and strength to the worshippers; and finally, it impinges on human consciousness with moral obligation. O'Dea goes on to suggest that this set of characteristics is remarkably similar to Rudolf Otto's analysis of the holy, the numinous experiences. It is remarkable because Durkheim is normally seen as a positivist, and yet here, his analysis of the sacred experience in life is described in more phenomenological terms, and with results very like those of more 'religious' phenomenologists such as Otto and G. van der Leeuw. For Otto the holy is not just the very good, but independent of our moral notions initially; and it is also non-rational. It is 'wholly other', quite beyond the usual, the intelligible and the familiar. What is involved is the 'element of majesty or absolute overpoweringness' and it evokes a 'peculiar dread' but is at the same time attractive and inviting to the beholder.

The coincidence of many strategic elements of the analysis of Durkheim's and Otto's treatment of the sacred, or holy, is worthy of our attention. These elements are the extraordinary character of the phenomenon, its implication of power, its ambiguity in relation to man, its awesome character and the feeling of dependence it arouses.[6]

This experience of the sacred is fundamental to organised religion, but the latter has ritualised the relationship with the sacred powers, the Holy, in ways which, as O'Dea has argued, can never be final. Yet religious experience tends to lead to the formation of specifically religious groups, partly through the process Max Weber termed the routinisation of charisma. The notion of 'charisma' is very closely linked with the idea of the 'sacred' and the 'holy' as outlined.[7] A person who has had a very fundamental religious experience or encounter with the holy may become the founder of a new religious group which may be contained within existing organisational frameworks, like Saint Francis, or lead to new organisations, such as happened with Luther, Calvin and John Wesley. The process of new religious groups emerging involves the idea of 'religious virtuosity' as Weber called the quality possessed by people with a peculiar 'ear' for the holy, and sacred experiences.[8] Such people will tend to develop a following in their own lifetime, which may or may not lead to a new and long-lasting religious organisation with its own rituals to evoke the peculiar religious experience with which the original founder was primarily concerned.

There are more studies of breakaway religious movements which later become organisations than of the ways such new experiences are contained within a Church. Catholics are more prone to remain within the church structures if possible than are Protestants, because they believe that the Church is not just a man-made organisation, but a sacred one, with the power to dispense grace through its sacraments. The Anglican Church sought to contain some religious virtuosi, and has been relatively more successful with those with a Catholic type of theology than with a Protestant one. When Newman left the Anglican Church, there was not a mass exodus of Anglo-Catholics, but rather a consolidation of the new ideas centring to some extent around Pusey. Joachim Wach's work contains a useful typology for examining the ways in which new charismatic movements can be contained within the Church—Ecclesiola in ecclesia is the main category for Protest movements within a Church, with three sub-categories: the Collegium pietatis; the Fraternitas; and the Monastic Order.[9]

The ritualists within the Church of England, and especially those with Socialist political views, were the most important recent example of such a movement in the last hundred years.[10] More recently there has been the liturgical movement, and the new theology of the Bishop of Woolwich, John Robinson, now in the University of Cambridge. This movement has been contained within the Church of England.

Many people in any society undergoing a large degree of social change, such as modern England, will find that the organised religious groups do not provide for their experience of the sacred, the holy dimension, assuming that they are in contact with it at all. In England there is still considerable use made of life-cycle rituals provided by the Church of England, and almost no one dies without some kind of religious ritual being performed after their death. Even the old who die without any known family are buried, or cremated, with a religious functionary performing a religious rite of burial. In other, more regular, forms of worship the social class differences between the people living in England are basic to the formation of congregations at specific churches, and in affecting who stays away from church altogether. Young people who have had drug experiences often turn to various forms of oriental religion, as more in keeping with their 'religious' experiences. Apart from this exception and obviously that of ethnic minorities, class differences seem to be the most important in England in creating such different values and ways of life, that worshipping together is not easy, or even possible. The Church of England is a Church of the upper classes and the middle classes, and very rarely do working-class people attend its regular services of worship. Where they do, it is in parishes with a sense of community among the working class themselves. Ordinary working people are the church wardens, and fill the other lay offices in such parishes. Where there are middle-class people in a parish, they will tend to dominate and fill the lay offices in the parish system, and the working-class people come to feel left out, and do not go regularly to the services.[11]

There are some ritual acts which are still central to Christianity, and which have not changed basically for at least two thousand years. The use of water at baptism is one such, which is discussed in the chapter on life-cycle rituals. The other basic act is that of taking bread and wine, blessing them in some way, and breaking and eating the bread and drinking the wine, among the members of the congregation.

Was ever another command so obeyed? For century after century, spreading slowly to every continent and country and among every race on earth, this action has been done, in every conceivable human circumstance, for every conceivable human need from infancy and before it to extreme old age and after it, from the pinnacles of earthly greatness to the refuge of fugitives in the caves and dens of the earth. Men have found no better thing than this to do for kings at their crowning and for criminals going to the scaffold; for armies in triumph or for a bride and bridegroom in a little country church; for the proclamation of a dogma or a good crop of wheat; for the wisdom of the Parliament of a mighty nation or for a sick old woman afraid to die; for schoolboy sitting an examination or for Columbus setting out to discover America; for the famine of whole provinces or for the soul of a dead lover; in thankfulness because my father did not die of pneumonia; for a village headman much tempted to return to fetich because the yams had failed; because the Turk was at the gates of Vienna; for the repentance of Margaret; for the settlement of a strike; for a son for a barren woman; for Captain so-and-so, wounded and prisoner of war; while the lions roared in the nearby amphitheatre; on the beach at Dunkirk; while the hiss of scythes in the thick June grass came faintly through the windows of the church; tremulously, by an old monk on the fiftieth anniversary of his vows; furtively, by an exiled bishop who had hewn timber all day in a prison camp near Murmansk; gorgeously for the canonisation of St Joan of Arc—one could fill many pages with the reasons why men have done this, and not tell a hundredth part of them. And best of all, week by week and month by month, on a hundred thousand successive Sundays, faithfully, unfailingly, across all the parishes of christendom, the pastors have done this just to make the *plebs Sancta Dei*— the holy common people of God.[12]

Theological interpretations of this act have varied, and still do, but the ritual seems to continue as basic to Christian groups. The actions surrounding it vary from time and place, but the basic act is usually recognisable. The central theological problem has been about the nature of the act, whether it is a new sacrifice each time it is done, or a remembrance of one sacrifice, that of Jesus. As Durkheim points out in his study of Australian aborigines' religion, '. . . *a sacrifice* is composed of two essential elements; an act of communion and an act of oblation. The worshipper communes with his god by taking in a sacred food, and at the same time he makes an offering to his god. We find these two acts in the Intichiuma . . .'[13] Given this as the definition of 'sacrifice', then the Anglican ritual of the Eucharist, or Holy Communion, is a sacrifice, for sociological purposes. It contains the two essential actions, the eating of sacred food in the actual communion itself, which is believed by some to be the body and blood of Christ present in some way in the bread and wine, and is thus an eating of a human sacrifice as well as a communion with God. The congregation also make an act of oblation, symbolised in the giving of money during the collection, and the offering of the bread and wine at the altar, which is often done by two members of the congregation to make the point clearer that the laity are giving these. The priest says, over these objects on the altar—'Pray, brethren, that this our sacrifice may be acceptable to God the Father Almighty'. The people: 'May the Lord accept the sacrifice to the praise and glory of His name for our good also, and for that of all His holy church'. (Series 2) And during the Prayer of Consecration—'And here we offer and present unto thee, O Lord, ourselves, our souls and bodies, to be a reasonable, holy and lively sacrifice unto thee: . . .'

This sacrificial act is the centre of the worship of the Christian Church, and has been for nearly two thousand years, and will

4 Priest consecrating bread and wine in the westward position, facing the congregation. Note the tabernacle behind the priest, where the consecrated bread is reserved.

5 Interior of the Shrine of the Holy House of Our Lady of Walsingham. Devotion was re-started in the Anglican Church at Walsingham in 1922.

Photograph by Kenneth Faircloth

6 Anglican clergy in the a[n]
Whit Monday pilgrimage t[o]
Holy House at Walsingha[m]

Photograph by Kenneth Faircloth

7 Anglican laity on the a[n]
pilgrimage to the Holy Hou[se]
Walsingham.

Photograph by Kenneth Fa[ircloth]

continue to be, no doubt, whatever the future of the organisations at present called the Church. Such ritual acts of sacrifice are extremely ancient, existing long before written, sacred texts, as can be seen from the Australian aborigine societies. There seems every reason for thinking that the same basic type of ritual act will continue in the future in most human societies. It may not be specifically Christian always, but the symbolism of sacrifice is basic to man's psychic life, and to his social life, as Durkheim maintained. There are civic rituals which attempt to motivate men to make sacrifices for a social group, such as the rallies of political movements, various expressions of nationalism, and army rituals. Civic rituals of this type are not, analytically, part of the sacred. Often, historically, they have been, of course, in that the Christian Church has been involved in persuading men to die for their country, or for a prince, or a group of rulers, as part of their duty to God, and their sacrifice to Him. Communist societies are able to motivate people without an appeal to the old gods, and it may be that neither Church nor Party can do this without people feeling motivated in some ways independently of such ideological appeals. The latter may serve rather as legitimating ideologies. Nevertheless, they are important, for without such legitimation it is difficult to keep up the momentum in a war, for example. Within Christianity there has always been a minority who have claimed that their allegiance to the faith does not allow them to kill anyone at all, and most societies have been forced to recognise this claim sooner or later. 'Sacrifice' in this context is interpreted by the believer to mean risking persecution for his pacifism.

Even communist societies have not been able to fully eradicate some sections of their populations from wanting to meet as a religious group to perform some act of sacrifice and worship. These meetings are potentially a threat to any totalitarian regime of the Western or Eastern blocs in Europe, for they can lead to values and action stemming from the religious group and its experiences which are contrary to those of the ruling élites in those societies.

Within Anglican Catholicism, there is a rite derived from both modern Roman Catholic sources and from the

F

pre-Reformation English Church, which is more clearly a *commemorative ritual* than the Eucharist, or Mass, which as has been said is a sacrifice.[14] *The Stations of the Cross* is a mythic drama, portrayed in pictures, of the events of the Founder's torture and death. It involves people moving from one station to another, praying at each of fourteen images of a scene from the Passion of Jesus. Such commemorative rites in Christianity are primarily religious rituals. There are civic rituals of a similar type, both of national heroes, such as Henry VIII, portrayed in a recent television series in England, and of a political party type, the most important case being Lenin in his tomb in Moscow and the ritual events which take place, such as pilgrimage, past his tomb.

Another set of rituals which have been revived by Anglican Catholics in the Church of England during this century, derive from their conception of the Real Presence of Christ in the consecrated bread, from the Eucharist. One central and controversial issue has centred around the *Reservation of the Blessed Sacrament*. When Anglican Catholic clergy first introduced it, the practice was condemned by bishops, unless it was for the purpose of communion of the sick.[15] However, many of the Anglican Catholics also introduced ritual acts of Adoration of the Blessed Sacrament, in a service called '*Benediction*' in which the congregation is blessed by the priest holding the bread, after a series of ritual devotions have been made in front of the tabernacle in which the bread is kept, with a light always in front of it. The practice of Reservation has spread quite widely within the Church of England in the last few decades; for example, in a cathedral in one of the areas used for participant observation for this study, the Reservation of the Sacrament has been introduced in the 1960s, and people pray in front of it, although there is no service of Benediction, which is considered theologically suspect. This is because it can lead people to attend Benedictions, rather than take communion at a Eucharist. (Sometimes Benediction is at a more convenient time, namely early evening, after Evensong. Roman Catholics can now go to Evening Mass, a practice not very widespread in Anglican churches at present, i.e. 1973.)

The Feast of Corpus Christi, with its procession of the Blessed Sacrament through the streets of the parish, was also introduced by clergy who were committed to the dogma of the Real Presence. This is a feast for Thanksgiving for the institution of the sacrament of Holy Communion which is not done on the Eve of Good Friday itself, for the ritual for Maundy Thursday is, if anything, the Washing of Feet.

Holy Communion or the Eucharist, as the central ritual act of Christianity, is worth examining further in terms of the effects it may have on the participants through its symbolism and emotional structure. It is partly a ritual in which people hear the Word of God, through the reading of the Bible, and through the sermon. The first part of the revised liturgy in the Church of England is termed the Ministry of the Word, followed by the other sections of the rite. The sermon is usually seen as a teaching situation, in which the congregation is taught something of the faith, based on the gospel of the day. This may be ethical in its orientation, or more 'spiritual'. Usually, though, there are implications from the gospel and the sermon, and sometimes in the epistle, and the lesson from the Old Testament when this is used, which are meant to affect people's behaviour in the world morally. There are here, therefore, the moral implications of the 'sacred' which Durkheim mentions as being one of the important consequences of worshippers' participation in the sacred area, through ritual.[16] This does not necessarily mean that people live up to their ideals and moral values but that they are guided by them, and by the preacher's interpretations to some extent. The value implications of the gospels are often seen in terms of middle-class radical-liberalism, in the churches where the most articulate preachers are heard. Full conservatism, like full-bodied socialism, is much rarer, but the latter is if anything growing as a political position among clergy.

The rest of the rite is concerned with the preparation of people, and the bread and wine, for the act of communion. At a Mass during which incense is used there is a point in the rite where the priests and congregations are censed, after the offertory and before the consecration section begins. This is a clear ritual act in which all the things, and people, involved in the ritual action to follow, are shown symbolically to be able to approach the 'sacred'. The ritual of censing is not essential; the prayers, and being present for the first section, seem enough to allow the people and clergy to contact the sacred. In some churches holy water is used at the beginning of the rite in a ritual called the Asperges, in which the priest walks through the congregation sprinkling them with holy water. Again this is not essential. The *confession* of sin by the congregation is. There is a public confession before the consecration and communion, and individuals in the Church of England may go for individual confession before the service if they wish. The rubric on confession is 'None must, all may, some should'. After either private or general confession, the people are blessed and forgiven their sins. They are thus able to be brought into contact with the sacred itself, the consecrated bread and wine, believed by the Catholic groups to be the Body and Blood of Christ; in some sense an instance of God incarnate in the world now. For some this is almost a literal truth, for others it is a more symbolic truth. In any case it is the most sacred ritual of the Church; the consecration, the breaking of the bread, and communion.

THE LITURGICAL YEAR

The Church's year divides into two; in the first section the major events in the life of Jesus are commemorated. The reading of the gospel can be seen as a *commemorative ritual* of the Founder of the group, in Durkheim's terms. Some believe that the events which are solemnly recited are timeless and are continually re-enacted by the Church. The year begins with a period of preparation for four weeks, Advent, during which the Four Last Things are traditionally contemplated—Death, Judgement, Heaven, and Hell. These are the basic eschatological themes of Christianity, concerned as they are with the end of time, and of the world. Then follow the Incarnation festivals, Christmas and Epiphany, in which the theme of God made Man, and God being shown to the world through Jesus' life, are contemplated. A theme which has become lost in Western Christianity is contained in the Creed of Saint Athanasius—

'Who although he be God and Man; yet his is not two, but one Christ; One: not by conversion of the Godhead into flesh; but by taking of the Manhood into God . . .' This creed is supposed to be used at Morning Prayer, Matins, on the main festivals of the Church, including Christmas Day. Jesus is portrayed in the main as God made Man, but much of the mythic themes of Christianity make more sense when the emphasis is placed on the taking of Manhood into God by Jesus. The Festival of the Ascension, the last event in the life of Jesus after his Death and Resurrection, is the most clear-cut symbolic representation of Manhood being taken into God. The central mythic theme of Christianity concerns, then, Man becoming God; a much more humanist and noble theme than has been stressed in the last few centuries by the Western Church. The stress has been more on man's sinfulness and need for redemption, certainly a theme in the myth, but not the only one.[17]

After Epiphany there is a pause in the cycle of great events, and then Lent starts, six weeks of fasting and preparation for the Death and Resurrection of Jesus in Holy Week. The rituals of this section of the Christian year are very rich and varied, especially during Holy Week itself. The liturgy of Good Friday involves, in Anglican Catholic Churches, *the Veneration of the Cross*, and the solemn intoning of the Passion according to Saint John. The cross is veiled in purple, no others are visible in the church; it is unveiled in three stages, first one arm, then the other, and finally the central piece. Then the congregation moves forward to kiss the unveiled cross with the figure of Christ on it. This is a very moving ritual, and works on a very unconscious level. There are various interpretations of the symbolism; in part it is veneration of wood and trees, a sacred tree. Such ritual is common in many societies outside Europe, and Christianity may have adapted an existing ritual of veneration of a sacred tree in this one of Good Friday. There is also the possibility of phallic worship, working on an unconscious level.[18] In Jungian terms the cross can also be a symbol of wholeness, based on the number four: + (a cross has four points). The ritual's meaning can be in part all these; the use of a crucifix, which is usual, is more than just a cross of wood. It is the final unveiling of the figure of Jesus on the cross which gives the ritual its climax, and a more sexual connotation than the Jungian interpretation allows for. Trees are complex symbols for they can be Mother symbols, when the image involves the leaves and branches overhanging in an enfolding way. However, the trunk of a tree, as used more in the cross symbol, is a more phallic symbol than this. The feminine is present in Catholic ritual in the symbolism of Mary.

The second section of the year involves examining events in the life of Jesus and of the Church. There are many festivals, usually not Sundays, which are festivals of the saints, or of Mary, or of the Church itself. The Sundays following Trinity Sunday in the Church of England lack specific rituals of their own.

The rituals used in connection with Mary are important, for they give a more feminine element to the ritual system, which is lacking in the ritual of more Protestant Anglican Churches. *The cult of Mary* is seen as very much a Roman Catholic aberration by many Anglicans, and only a minority of Anglican Churches in England have developed it to any great extent. Those that have are very Catholic oriented. The interest in the role of Mary in Christian myth is growing among all Anglicans, and even among Free Churchmen. This looks as though it will continue, as it has since the end of the Second World War, to develop the mothering aspects of the Church, and the feminine elements in the myth, and no doubt, as a consequence, in the members of the congregations. After the Puritan destruction of the images of Mary in England during the Reformation, only the name remained in the Church of England's churches—'The Church of the Virgin Mary'. The statues were broken, the pictures first disappeared, and some slowly came back for decoration, not for devotional purposes. Almost no members of the Church of England used the Rosary after the Reformation, until this century. The Angelus was not rung in the Anglican churches after the Reformation period. Some Anglican Catholic churches now ring the Angelus regularly, especially if there is a religious order of monks or nuns attached to the church. The bell is a *signal* to pray, and is not highly symbolic itself.

The Shrine of Our Lady at Walsingham was a major one in

mediaeval Europe. It was re-established by the Anglican Church in 1922 and a new Holy House built between 1931-38, and it is now a growing centre for ritual devotion to Mary in the Church of England. There is an attempt being made to revive other shrines of Our Lady, and one in Willesden may well open during the 1970s. People go on a pilgrimage to Walsingham and take water from the holy well, which has no medicinal qualities of the kind found at spas, nor is it holy water, but water blessed by the Church, and used for sick people to drink, or have sprinkled on them. Cures do take place as a result of this. The Walsingham phenomenon is similar to Lourdes, but on a much smaller scale. The Rosary is a circle of fifty-four beads, with an additional five beads and a crucifix attached. The beads are for counting the 'Hail Mary' prayers, and the larger ones for the 'Our Father'. There are five sections of ten beads each. The full set of meditations for the Rosary involves going round the beads three times in all. The first round for the Joyful Mysteries, concerned with the events leading up to the birth of Jesus and his childhood; the second for the Sorrowful Mysteries, concerned with the Passion and Crucifixion; and the third for the Glorious Mysteries concerned with the Resurrection and Ascension of Jesus, the Assumption and Coronation of Mary as Queen of Heaven.[19]

Why has this renewal of the rituals around the symbol of Mary taken place in this century? The answer is difficult to establish, but there are both general and more particular reasons which can be offered. In general terms in can be seen as an aspect of the process of 'feminisation' of culture which has occurred in England since the end of the phase of imperialist expansion in the nineteenth century and the wars of the twentieth century. World wars tend to 'masculinise' the culture in terms of putting a high value on fighting, aggression, and physical prowess among males. Nevertheless there has also been the growth of sub-cultural areas where this has not occurred, most importantly among pacifist groups such as the Quakers, and the Anglican Pacifist Fellowship, and among artists and intellectuals who were appalled by the First World War especially—Wilfred Owen, Bertrand Russell, Siegfried

Sassoon.[20] Later the Campaign for Nuclear Disarmament during the late fifties and early sixties also marked a large growth of the anti-war movement among middle-class people.[21] In the world of pop music, too, there is a shift to a different image of the male ideal which has grown up during the 1960s. It even affects footballers, both their image, and their behaviour as players on the field.[22] There has been a growing number of people in the middle and working classes, where the stress on the highly agressive male, as the ideal, has lessened. At the same time, the use of women in the factories and the professions has grown, particularly since the Second World War, and thus the position of women has changed to some extent, and their contribution to society is more acknowledged. The legacy of two world wars has been to enhance the position of women, to lead to the growth of anti-war sentiments, but also to a reinforcement of the ideal of the highly aggressive male. This latter has only been challenged in the last decade. Given this situation it is not surprising that some Anglican Catholics have been able, and willing, to revive ritual veneration of Mary as a central feminine symbol in Christianity. The general socio-cultural setting was one which supported such sentiments more than was the case in the nineteenth century, when the Anglican Catholic movement and ritualism began.

More specifically within the Church of England, a pluralist position began to emerge as the Church lost full uniformity in its ritual and theology, after the growth of the Catholic movement. The Anglican Catholics possessed a coherence, however, previously lacking in Anglican thought, and it captured the imagination of intelligent and creative clergy and laity. There has therefore been a consistent shift towards the 'Catholic' end of the spectrum, in both thinking and ritual practice, since the end of the nineteenth century. First one area, then another, of the Church's ritual practices have been altered, or extended, to include more 'Catholic' practices, and thus the rituals of Mary fit in this context of the gradual assimilation of more and more of the rituals of the English Catholic Church before the Reformation, and of the modern Roman Catholic and Eastern Orthodox Churches.

ORDINATION AND REUNION SCHEMES

The *rite de passage* of *Ordination* serves to set apart a group of people, priests, for special purposes. These are to administer the sacraments, to preach, and to minister to the people in their congregation and parishes. Priests in the West are usually full-time, but some do have other occupations such as teaching. Essentially the ritual of Ordination is a 'negative rite' in Durkheim's terms, in that it sets apart people who will have special positive relations with the sacred, in this case the sacraments, especially the Eucharist and Confession, with the power to absolve people from sin. Protestant Churches stress the preaching aspect almost entirely, and their clergy are not seen as priests who have special sacramental power in relation to either the Mass, nor in relation to the absolution of sins in Confession. Within the Church of England, there is a compromise between the Protestant and the Roman Catholic position, in that the role of the priest is retained, primarily in relation to Holy Communion, for only an ordained priest can perform the ritual of consecration of the bread, wine and water. The role of the priest as confessor towards individual penitents is much less developed than in the Roman Catholic Churches. Only the Anglo-Catholics have tried to develop Confession, and absolution, in a way comparable to the Roman Church. The Eastern Orthodox Churches also have developed the sacrament of individual confession to a greater degree than the typical Church of England parish, even an Anglo-Catholic one. It is these two sacraments which most differentiate 'Catholic' priests in any of the Churches from Protestant ones, for the latter, like the former, may perform Baptism, Marriage, and Burial rites. It is this difference that led some Anglo-Catholic theologians to develop the notion of 'Apostolic Succession' and to apply it to the clergy in the Roman Catholic Church, the Eastern Orthodox Churches, and the Anglican Church, but not to the Protestant Churches. The power to consecrate the sacred elements in the Mass, and to absolve penitents from sins, is believed to be given during the rite of Ordination, when this is performed by a bishop who has himself been consecrated by other bishops within the Apostolic

Succession. This is an example of what Max Weber called the 'routinisation of Charisma', in that the charisma of Christ was given by Him to His apostles, who in turn transmitted it to others in a special ritual act involving the laying on of hands by a person in possession of the charisma.[23] The idea of Apostolic Succession is not always understood in a purely mechanistic way, but it seems to require both subjective intention on the part of the bishops and persons being ordained to give and receive the charisma, and an objective component, that the bishops performing the ordination really are in a direct line with the first bishops, and, therefore, the apostles. It is this last component which led the Roman Church to deny validity to the bishops of the Church of England, and therefore to its priests, in a Papal Bull of 1896. The Eastern Orthodox Church has recognised Anglican Orders, i.e. its bishops, priests and deacons, to be within the Apostolic Succession. The Roman Catholic Church has recognised the validity of the Eastern Orthodox Churches' Orders (*N.B.* these priests may marry). It is presumably only a matter of time before the Roman Church will find a way of recognising the validity of Anglican Orders.[24]

The issue is complicated by the negotiations between the Church of England and the Methodist Church, for there is a problem about the subjective intentions of some Methodist ministers in 'receiving Episcopacy into their system'. Some Anglicans, both clergy and laity, were worried about whether they really intended to be in Apostolic Succession as Catholics understand this.[25] This led to the rejection of the Scheme for Unity between the Church of England and the Methodist Church in 1972 by a substantial minority of both clergy and laity, sufficient to cause the scheme to be dropped. At the time the mass media seemed to report this decision as meaning that another nail had been put into the coffin for the organised Churches, revealing the dislike of church religion held by many reporters in the Press and television.

From a sociological perspective it appears rather more understandable, and much less threatening to the organised Churches. It is understandable because throughout this century the more 'Catholic' understanding of the priest's role has been growing in the Church of England among laity and clergy. This process cannot be reversed in a sudden way to meet the fashion of the 1960s for schemes of Reunion, which were most popular among the full-time preofessions of the Churches rather than many of the older laity.

The division between the more 'Catholic' understanding and 'Protestant' one among ordinary laity of the various Churches is not one which is easily altered in matters like this, for it has to do with the nature of the 'sacred' in their rituals. It would be potentially polluting to allow people who were not regarding themselves, and not regarded by others, as really being in Apostolic Succession, to celebrate Mass, or to claim to forgive sins.[26] In this area of the sacred, strong emotions are bound to be aroused if there is the suggestion that people who are not properly, ritually, prepared are allowed to perform sacred ritual acts. The professionals may feel this less than the laity, for being involved full-time with the sacred dimension may well lessen the degree of awe in which it is approached, compared with the more segmental involvement of the laity, for whom the sacred dimension is more awful precisely because it is more separated off from the profane affairs of earning a living and rearing a family.

If the scheme had gone through because not enough of the representatives of the hard line on the sacred nature of Apostolic Succession had been present at the decision-making meeting, then there would most probably have been further splits, even leading to the formation of three religious organisations, where previously there had been only two. For the Anglo-Catholics may have tried to keep their separateness, so might the extremely Protestant Methodists, and the third and largest group would have been the co-operating Anglicans and Methodists. Yet in this situation all three organisations could well have been weakened by the splits. Schemes for Reunion in the heartlands of Christianity, especially in Europe, rather than India or Africa, are likely to weaken the existing organisations rather than strengthen them, as could occur in societies where all Christians are a relatively new minority group who have more in common with one another because other religions are the main base of religious differentiation. In Europe it is the various denominations of Christianity which reflect the class and status groups' struggles of centuries, and this is why the divisions cannot be so easily healed, as they can in India, for example. The easy assumption made by many reports that the dropping of the scheme for reunion between the Church of England and the Methodists would weaken organised religion was more probably the opposite of the reality of what might have happened. Religious organisations, because they handle different classes and status 'groups' conceptions of the sacred and its relations with the profane, cannot be treated as though they were industrial firms 'ripe' for some other group to take over. Yet it is to be expected that the specialists in the Churches, the clergy, would reflect these assumptions given their situation. They are under social and cultural pressures to appear up-to-date and relevant in their work, and tend to adopt the values and ideas of the other full-time managers of large organisations. It is this process which is the real threat to religious organisations, for many laity perceive the Church as a 'sacred' organisation, set apart from profane affairs. If the 'managers' of the Churches adapt too much to profane organisational methods it is likely that more and more laity will look to other religious movements for the sacred experiences they seek at the moment in church.[27]

ANGLICAN RITUALS AND ENGLISH CAPITALISM

Are religious rituals on the 'way out'? In an advanced industrial society can they still communicate anything to people? Clearly there are still substantial minority groups in modern England who are socialised into an understanding of them, or an emotional attachment to them. This will no doubt continue to be the case for the next few generations at least, for such patterns are rooted in families who attend church rituals and teach their children about the Church. There has probably never been a time when the majority of the English population attended Church of England services regularly; it has always been a minority who were really dedicated to Anglicanism at any period. Attendances by people seeking entertainment will obviously have dropped given radio, cinema, television and mass sporting events. It should not be forgotten, however, that even so the Church has face-to-face contact in its social events, and this is still important in drawing people into groups, instead of the isolation of watching television and cinema screens. The Church of England is still the Church nearly two-thirds of English people turn to for some civic or life-cycle ritual events. The numbers of those who follow its religious ritual and its liturgical year is probably small, but not significantly falling. The numbers of Easter communicants is a good measure of dedicated Anglicans, because it is a minimum ritual duty laid down by the Church of England for its members, and is clearly a religious ritual *par excellence*. The numbers here have risen overall, but fallen as a proportion of the total population. In 1900 there were 93 per 1,000 of population receiving communion on Easter Day; in 1920 the figure was 88; in 1940 it was 63 per 1,000; in 1950 it was 58; in 1960 it was 65; and in 1968 it was 56.[28]

In that it can be safely asserted that most English people do not regard church attendance as crucial to their claim to be Christian, the ritual symbolic system of the Church of England can be said to fail to communicate with the majority. However, it is doubtful if changing the ritual and symbols in any radical way would have much effect on this, because the failure of the Church to involve the majority is not basically caused by the nature of the rituals, symbols and myths themselves as by the position of the Church of England in the English class system. It is linked more than any Church with ruling class families, although less than it used to be. Figures in this area, like others, can be difficult to interpret. D. H. J. Morgan's study of the background of Anglican bishops, for instance, shows a real decline in number of bishops who come directly from aristocratic ruling class families, from 33 per cent between 1860 and 1879 to 2 per cent between 1940 and 1960. The number from homes where the father was a clergyman has risen from 18 per cent in the 1860-79 period to 48 per cent in 1940-59 and 54 per cent in 1960. What is not shown is where these clerical families which produce bishops were located in the class structure in the last generation. Bishops still attend public schools and Oxbridge universities. In 1960 85 per cent of the bishops had been at public school; 89 per cent had been to Oxbridge.[29] The Anglican bishops in England tend to represent the values and attitudes of the upper and upper-middle classes in England.

At parish level the clergyman is often nearer middle and upper-working class people than any bishop in terms of his experience, but may be removed from them by education—by no means a unique situation for professional people. The local congregation may be predominantly middle class in composition, and its values and cliques will reflect this. So many working-class people feel the church is not for them; they may feel excluded and uncomfortable in the presence of middle-class members of the Church of England. This factor, in large part, makes for lack of attendance, rather than any intrinsic problem with the rituals as such. The ritual system of Anglican Catholicism was attractive to working-class people when presented to them by a priest without too many middle-class attitudes and assumptions, especially about the Labour Party and the trade unions. It is the relation between the working class and the middle classes, under capitalist economic conditions, which produces this discontinuity and polarisation in a society such as England. The Church is ill-equipped to bridge it because it is seen as part of the upper middle class institutions for governing. Its values and attitudes have for too long been moulded by the need to legitimate the ruling capitalist classes in England, and to be not too critical towards their actions in political, military and economic affairs. Socialists have always been a minority voice in the Church of England, although a significant one in terms of the consistency with which the political implications of Christianity were traced out to lead to a form of real socialism, involving real public ownership and control. The Church of England as a whole could never accept this set of implications and still legitimate the capitalist rulers in England, and, therefore, it compromised on its values and teachings with regard to political and economic affairs. Its rituals became so much the less meaningful, the more the official statements and values, derived supposedly from the gospel, were legitimating British capitalism. The implications of the values contained in the gospel, and in the rituals of the Church, clearly lead, it seems to me, to a solid form of socialism (i.e. not social democracy within modern capitalism). The Church is supposed to be seeking to unite all men and women; this is especially true of the 'Catholic' type of teaching, for 'Catholic' we are told means 'universal'. Yet Britain has acted, and continues to act, in ways which hardly make for common aspirations among the peoples of the world at large. Britain, especially under Tory governments, pursues policies both at home and abroad based on inequalities between classes, nations, and races. These inequalities are assumed to be acceptable, and in need of no real fundamental changes, because they make for efficiency. The history which suggests that such inequalities lead to political unrest, violence, crime and wars is ignored.

One factor which may well influence the attitudes of church leaders to political and economic issues in Britain and elsewhere in the world is the fact that the Church of England owns large amounts of capital itself. In 1971 the Church of England held investments to the value of £500 million. This was held in various forms of investment, including property, excluding the value of church buildings themselves. The Methodist Church, in the same year, held investments and deposits to the value of £8 million only. Given this situation it is highly probable that the Church of England will survive no matter how many people attend its services—short of revolutionary confiscation of its wealth. This enormous wealth has built up over centuries and is clearly an embarrassment to some Anglican Christians. Nevertheless, on the whole it gives the Church a considerable stake in modern capitalism.[30]

However, those in the Church who seek a more equalitarian world system, and who make a connection between international capitalism and the lack of peace in the world, tend to become more critical of the Church of England's role in legitimating Britain's place in the capitalist system.

CONCLUSION

It may be that Christian theology implies that the sacred should be made to disappear, as some theologians claim, but this is not the main issue here. Rather it is to understand why the sacred dimension of experience seems necessary in human societies, and what is likely to happen in conditions where the historical religious organisations cease to provide such experience for some people.

The sacred dimension develops in society when people are distressed in some way, through sickness, death, natural disasters, or man-made disasters such as war or economic depressions. Equally it can develop when people feel profoundly thankful and joyful, after the birth of a child for example, or on a beautiful day, or after an experience of creativity. It is primarily to do with human feelings and emotions, rather than intellectual beliefs or moral values. It is certainly related to these, but is analytically and even empirically distinguishable from them. People in a similar occupation, and with similar life experiences, will tend to develop similar conceptions of the sacred.

Max Weber understood this, and documented some of the important historical examples in the major world religions. People set up movements and organisations to develop rituals which have a capacity to arouse in them as a group an experience of the sacred which they find meaningful. If a group of specialists emerges in these organisations they will tend to become removed from the life-experiences of their congregations, except in middle-class areas perhaps. The laity may become confused about new ideas and rituals introduced by the specialists, for they may be such as to cease to arouse the sacred dimension for the laity.[31] The laity may then become apathetic, attend less, or not at all, or they form a new religious movement, such as Pentecostalism, or as in the case with some young people, move into a cult or sect of an Oriental religion, which they can influence so that it suits their conception of sacred experiences. There is, therefore, a tendency towards anti-clerical movements in religious organisations, whenever there is rapid socio-cultural and economic change occurring. Under stable conditions, the religious specialists do not appear to some to be out of date, they are under less pressure to adapt to dominant new élites in the society. They can have a continuity of religious experience with their congregations under such conditions. Once change begins new groups emerge, the religious specialists become more and more isolated from many groups in their congregations, and begin to form their own professional identity. This is the point at which laity are likely to assert themselves in some way, which in the extreme will mean leaving the old organisation and forming a new one, perhaps even forming a new religion outside the main historical religion of the area. To some young people in Africa or India, Christianity has appeared 'modern'; to some young people in Europe and America in the 1960s and 1970s, Hinduism and Buddhism, or the esoteric side of Islam as in Sufism, are attractive. Christianity seems barren, and cannot provide sacred experiences in a way these old Asian religions, when adapted, are able to do.[32]

G

Chapter Five

Nationalism and Civic Ritual

Modern nation states are involved in trying to instil into their populations feelings of national identity. To do this they use ritual occasions, among other techniques. The use of the educational system for instilling notions of nationalism is often of central importance in societies building up such an identity for the first time, as in the new countries which have emerged in Africa since the end of Second World War, as well as in societies which have a longer established national identity. It is also important to see that such feelings of identity are not just the result of manipulation of non-élites by some ruling power group, for often a group may feel they are a separate national group, although attempts may be being made to integrate them into a larger national state, which may be dominated by another group. There are numerous examples of this in contemprary societies, for example in Yugoslavia, the USSR, America where the blacks feel a separate group and Northern Ireland where the Irish Catholics feel a separate minority group.

It may be the case that rituals both help to express feelings of nationalism, to further develop them, and instil them into new generations. They may also make some groups feel less part of the national group in that they are made conscious of the fact that they do not share some of the values which seem to lie behind the group's ritual. For example, there has always been a small but significant group in Britain who feel this way when they witness rituals involving the Royal Family. There are numerous examples, but Trooping the Colour on the Queen's official birthday, the speech of the sovereign on Christmas Day, or the State Opening of Parliament, are all ritual occasions in which some groups, such as radical youth, find their sense of separateness from the main society reinforced. The main reason for these feelings of separateness arises from the values and way of life implicit in the ritual, such as respect for established authority, and military virtues.

The predominant form of political civic ritual in the modern world, and certainly including industrial societies, are the rituals of nationalism. This seems to be so because national identity depends almost wholly on the symbolic level for its maintenance. This has been successful to such a degree that most people seem to believe in the 'naturalness' of nations. At some fundamental level, people in industrial societies seem to use nationality as a base for their sense of identity, and for making some sense and meaning out of the flux of their experiences. Crucial to this sense of national identity is the idea of history; history is largely written in terms of nations. The new nations of Africa, for example, embarked on a major exercise of writing their own national histories, during the 1950s and 1960s, and this seemed to be an essential part of developing a sense of national identity. The history was written by university researchers, then used in simplified form in the schools, so that a new generation of children would grow up with some implicit notion of national identity. The history lessons, both in Africa and also in industrial societies, take on more life if they are made more dramatic, either in the form of films, or theatre events, about the history of the nation, or in the form of national ritual occasions, such as the Nations' Independence Day celebrations, or an anniversary of a battle, such as the Battle of Britain, or Anzac Day in Australia. These events will centre around a national leader, who may be the political head of state, such as a president, or a monarch. In industrial societies, television plays an important role in transmitting the central event to the homes of millions of viewers, who may or may not actually take part in the local manifestation of the occasion, e.g. Remembrance Day services.

There is ritual wherever political office is held, and where law is made or executed, as in the Courts. This has the function of impressing upon the office holder that he is to regard himself as a member of the nation, or smaller political unit such as a city, and to rule and administer laws for the interests of the unit, and not for his own interests. This may explain in part why business-men never carry the same ritualised charisma with them as do political figures or lawyers, for they are allowed to administer and rule their organisations in their own interests, at least this is the case under entrepreneurial capitalism.[1] Where the business moves towards a different orientation, so might one expect ritual to develop around key office holders. Quite apart from the effect of ritual on the office holder himself, there is more importantly, perhaps, the function for the group as a whole. Because the office holder is supposed to be the bearer of the group's identity and interests, and not just his own, he, as leader and office holder, can expect loyalty from the members of the group. They may even have to follow his orders to fight for the group. This loyalty may be explicitly mentioned in speeches at ritual occasions involving the office holder's presence, or it may be present in special songs and anthems, sung by all present, e.g. The Red Flag, national anthems.

THE CHURCH OF ENGLAND AND POLITICAL RITUAL

It seems advisable to give special attention to the Church of England in the present context, because it is still the dominant Christian organisation constitutionally, given the position of the Crown as head of the Church, the position of the Arch-bishop of Canterbury in the Coronation ceremony, and the fact that it remains the Established Church in England.

The Church of England provides an interesting case study in terms of the complex connections between political, national, and religious rituals. Here comparison with groups of Christians who are English (not, for example, Irish, Italian, Greek, or Scots) but who attend either rituals of the Roman Catholic or Free Churches, would be useful in understanding the meaning of ritual action for people who maintain an English national identity without being C. of E. It is difficult, however, to cover all the various ritual groups that exist within Britain given the type of method which is being followed in this study. For every religious and ethnic group, each social class and youth group, would require at least a year of close study, and in the case of the large groups such as the Roman Catholics, some years' work would be necessary.

During the twentieth century the Church of England has continued to be the nationally established Church, with the monarch remaining head of state, and head of the Church of England. This connection began during the rise of the modern nation-state in England, when the political authority of the Pope was under question by the newly emerging English ruling class during the sixteenth century. At this stage there was a close connection between religion and political allegiance, so that, with the Elizabethan settlement, the link between the Church of England and English nationalism was firmly established. All Englishmen born into the nation state of England were, *ipso facto*, members of the Church of England, with its attempt to be comprehensive enough to contain a variety of theological viewpoints from moderate Catholic to moderate Puritan. Although this attempt was never entirely successful, because there was not one nation with one set of economic and political interests and, therefore, no one religious body which could express these, it did leave the continuing legacy of the link between English national identity and the Church of England.

In a most recent report on the relations of Church and State, from the Archbishop's Commission of 1970, it was reported, on the basis of evidence submitted to them by many other Church leaders and other interested organisations, that *the Coronation* was an important symbol for many people outside the Church of England, as well as for most in that Church.

The representatives of our Church who agreed with representatives of the Methodist Church in framing a scheme for unity, were able to agree in hoping that the Sovereign would continue to have a special place in any united Church.

So far as we can ascertain, the place of the Sovereign, as a symbol of national recognition and encouragement, gives rise to very little difficulty, is seldom resented by non-Christians, would not be an obstacle to Christian unity, and is much valued by many persons.

We hope that other Churches will be brought, in a more formal way than hitherto, into the rites of Coronation. The rite itself may need further substantial adaptation to meet the times, which we hope to be distant times.[2]

In 1970, therefore, a situation existed in which the position of the sovereign in the Established Church was one valued by people who were estranged from the Church of England.

There is an interesting emphasis in the above quotation from the report, on having the sovereign encourage and recognise the Christian Church, but no mention of the other aspect, probably more significant, that of the Christian Church (Anglican or United) legitimating the nation state of England, and its existing constitution.

Edward Shils and Michael Young wrote an interesting account of the meaning of the Coronation of Elizabeth II in 1953 (their paper was published in 1953).[3] They saw the Coronation as a ritual of communion, bringing the whole nation into a ritualistic dedication to the basic values of the society. The values they instance are: generosity, charity, loyalty, justice in the distribution of opportunities and rewards, reasonable respect for authority, and respect for the individual and his freedom. The sovereign is brought into contact with these sacred values in the rite, and they are seen to be over and above the person of the sovereign in the ritual actions of the Coronation, such as the presenting of the Holy Bible to her as God's Laws, and her standing in frail clothing, without the robes of royal office, at an early point in the ritual. Shils and Young's analysis makes clear that many of the population were deeply involved in the ritual, and see it as the expression of the people's commitment to the sacred values. The ritual also handles the emotional ambivalence that people have towards moral authority and moral rules. There is no hint, however, of any group whose ambivalence is based on the fact that they disagree with some of the values, or the way they are being interpreted. For example, the value they instance of 'justice in the distribution of opportunities and rewards' is ambiguously worded, but it would seem that even in the euphoria of the Coronation not all were agreed that the actual distribution of rewards was just, although no doubt adhering to the generalised value that justice in the distribution of rewards was desirable. Looking at this analysis two decades later, it seems that Shils and Young were themselves carried away by the seemingly overwhelming consensus about basic British values, and the worth of the society in the early 1950s. They instance the outcry over a cartoon David Low drew for *The Guardian* the day after the Coronation, to show that apart from a few of the intellectuals, all were agreed on the sacredness of the values and the rituals. Their paper ends with an historical perspective, pointing out that the monarch was not always so popular as in 1952, and that this popularity was due to the high degree of consensus over values in Britain at this period. This included many intellectuals too. They point out that the Coronation, like Christmas, was a family event, expressing the importance of the bonds of the family even under urban conditions. The days of intellectual critique of the family by people such as Havelock Ellis, Shaw, Russell, Lawrence, were over, they thought. This was written before the works by Ronald Laing and David Cooper, Juliet Mitchell and Germaine Greer, appeared during the late sixties, all of whom were critical of the family in perhaps even more fundamental terms than the earlier generation had been. The period of high consensus in Britain was short lived. In part it had built up during the Second World War, but was probabily not as high as Shils and Young thought even in the Coronation period.

Shils and Young draw on Emile Durkheim in their analysis of the Coronation, and ignore Max Weber and Karl Marx. They do not see that the Coronation, and other rituals surrounding the Royal Family, such as the giving of honours and decorations, the State Opening of Parliament, serve to legitimate the existing set of families who rule economically, politically (including the newer Labour families) and militarily. Yet William Bagehot saw that this was the case, and Shils and Young quote him, without drawing the conclusion that little has altered, except that the ruling families may number more than 10,000 individuals in this century. The monarchy enabled the educated 10,000 to go on governing as before. By commanding their unbounded loyalty, it 'tamed the uncouth labourers of Somersetshire who, in their simplicity, needed a person to symbolise the State'. In this way 'the English Monarchy strengthens our government with the strength of religion. . . . It gives now a vast strength to the entire constitution, by enlisting on its behalf the credulous obedience of enormous masses.'[4] The rituals surrounding the Royal Family and the rituals which involve the monarch, such as the Christmas Day broadcast, all serve to legitimate the economic and political *status quo*. Shils and Young's analysis would agree with this point. However, they must see it as a just system, as well as assuming that the vast majority of the English, let alone Scots, Welsh, and Northern Irish, populations also see it as just, and in need of little change. The last twenty years of research have shown that there is not as much justice in the opportunity structure as many assumed, or still assume.[5] The reward structure, whatever else it is, is clearly not erected on lines of justice which all accept. For if it were then there would be little problem in arranging an Incomes Policy acceptable to all major groups of workers in the society. The distribution of wealth remains very unequal, with 7 per cent of the population owning 85 per cent of invested wealth, 93 per cent sharing the remaining 15 per cent of invested wealth.[6] Given these inequalities it is not really surprising that 'the Coronation consensus' was somewhat ephemeral. Having said this, however, it is important to see that so far, apart from Northern Ireland, the disprivileged groups have not tried to alter the situation by violent means, although unconstitutional means are sometimes used. Here the degree of successful legitimation of the English Constitution shows itself. This is dependent on both a reasonable economic performance, such that a majority of working-class people feel better off, and on the success of the rituals of legitimation. The Royal Family, and the associated rites, do help stabilise the society, and have so far (1973) helped in preventing very violent attempts at change.

Given all this, the position of Socialists within the Church of England is somewhat problematic, for they see their Church being used in part to legitimate a political and economic system they regard as unjust, from the point of view of Christian moral and political theology. They are led to seek disestablishment as one way of lessening the degree of legitimation the present Establishment system gives to the rulers of Britain. The Church of England has, during this century, played no small part in legitimating the Labour Party and trade union movement into the British system. Christian Socialists are now left with the problem of how far, by doing this, they have compromised Socialism, so that the Labour Party in office now administers a mixed economy, but one nonetheless predominantly capitalist in nature.[7]

For others, the Church of England is a 'national institution' which expresses England's commitment to being a 'Christian' society. To separate the Church of England from the State *in toto* would for these people be tantamount to declaring that Britain was not a Christian country, and was no longer trying to be so, by seeming to repudiate the values of Christianity. The role of the Coronation ritual shows also the potentially profound constitutional problems which could emerge, not just at a purely legal level, but at the level of the feelings of legitimacy that the Constitution has for many English people. Church–State relations have been radically severed only in revolutionary situations, and it is not perhaps surprising that the attempts to get piecemeal reform of the situation are not meeting with quite the easy success many people, both in the Church of England and entirely outside it, imagined would be possible. The issues being raised bring out the ways in which the English Constitution is legitimated for many status groups in England.[8] The Constitution is made legitimate by being brought into contact with the sacred;[9] for many English people the fact that they think the Constitution and the country, therefore, is committed to Christian values is of crucial importance.[10] Few people, either clergy or laity, see the situation as one where the Constitution is designed to perpetuate the rule of the bourgeoisie of liberal, reformed capitalism, or in times of economic crisis, right-wing capitalism.

Yet historically this is the situation, from the time of the Restoration in 1660. As long as this situation continues, then so long will it be difficult to basically alter the relation of the Church and the State through the Crown. If, in the future, the Church of England united with Churches other than the Methodists, who are, one might say, 'deviant' Anglicans anyway, then this new Church will no doubt play a similar role to that of the Church of England in legitimating the Constitution, and of continuing the implied teaching that modern capitalism and Christianity are compatible in the world as a whole. No doubt a minority will continue to assert that this is not the case, that some form of Socialism is the only form of economic and political government which will eradicate poverty in the world, prevent exploitative pollution of the world's resources, and prevent wars of the kind produced by the needs of capitalism to be able to exploit labour and raw materials, and to find markets for its goods, including weapons of war themselves. These groups continue to assert that capitalism does not lead to a Christian way of life, but until capitalism disappears they will remain a minority. They will no doubt continue to work for disestablishment of the Church of England if they are Anglicans, as a way of sharpening the issue of how far the Church should be controlled by a State which is pursuing unchristian policies in many of its actions.[11]

The upsurge in the popularity of the monarchy in England reached its clearest peak in the 1950s, especially at the time of the Coronation. Since then it has been less marked as a phenomenon, but no doubt if there were a national crisis, the symbolism of the monarchy would re-emerge as one of the major symbols of English nationalism. The Church of England can also find that it is itself part of this basic, latent nationalism, and this makes it very difficult for the Church to take clear stands which are critical of the economic and political *status quo*. The Church of England tends to seek to express a set of core values which overarch the disputes and conflicts in the society, and so to act as a 'reconciler' between disputing parties. The church leaders are most likely to speak out in favour of seeking consensus than in pursuing economic justice through, for example, industrial conflict. The monthly diocesan letters of Anglican bishops, which are circulated to many irregular church attenders as well as to the more devoted members, are one of the prime means by which this is done. They can also make speeches, either in the House of Lords, or in Synod, or even in a sermon. Very few of these sources reveal that the bishops are either coherently committed Socialists or Tories. They represent what they see as reasonably liberal, middle-ground opinions. This preserves their positions as leaders of opinion on the Church quite satisfactorily during periods of relative social and economic peace. During more conflict-ridden periods, such as that of the Heath Government of the early seventies, their pronouncements are either innocuous, or anti-working class. A few are pro the working classes, and critical of profit and the market as a means of attaining a good society.[12]

Here is an example from a diocesan letter in an area under study for the purposes of research into Anglicanism in England. It was written in April 1972 at a time of high unemployment (over a million in March) and just after the end of the great national miners' strike of early 1972.

. . . the major political parties endlessly debating the details of policies which both in principle have accepted and *refusing to join together* [italics mine—R. B.] to wrestle with such matters as unemployment or the threat of world population or pollution which arise not so much from political policies as techno-logical developments.[13]

One of the problems for the Church of England is the way in which bishops are chosen—for until the Church alters its relation with the State they are chosen by the sovereign, on the advice of the prime minister. The prime minister usually has other things to think about and he takes the advice of one of the permanent civil servants attached to Number 10 Downing Street. He no doubt sounds out opinion among the other bishops already appointed in the Church. The result of this somewhat obscure process is that the bishops who do emerge are typically 'safe' both politically and theologically. They are not too extreme in either way. The dioceses have no real right to say 'No' to a suggested appointment. As the Church of England seeks to unite with other Churches, in some way or other, the role of the prime minister in appointing bishops becomes a real problem. The Howick Commission in 1964 reported that the role of the prime minister in this matter should continue, but since then representatives of the Roman Catholic and Free Churches have objected. The report of the Archbishop's Commission on 'Church and State' reported in 1970 that it was divided, some wanting to retain the part of the prime minister, and others wanting a form of election by members of the Church itself.[14]

This issue is an example of the difficulties of unity over any proposals for radical change in the existing relation of the Church of England and the State. The Church of England contains both traditionalists in these matters and those who seek change. These differences do not entirely coincide with theological differences. What is of interest at this point is that as the law stands at present, Parliament has authority to reject changes in the religious ritual of the Church of England, and it used this in 1927 and 1928 to prevent the 1928 prayer book being lawfully sanctioned. This did not prevent some of the new prayer book being used, however. In 1965 Parliament granted permission for new forms of worship to be tried in the Church of England for an experimental period. This period lasts until 1980. Then the problem will arise again of who decides the form of worship, and the doctrines of the Church of England, Parliament, or the Anglicans themselves, in their own governmental structure of the Church.

The root of the difficulty is that any attempt to change the relation between the Church and the State raises more fundamental problems about the ritual affairs of the nation than at first seem present. The central problem relates to the difference between the actively committed 'Anglicans' among the laity, and the less active members of the Church of England who regard themselves as 'C. of E.' and who use its services occasionally. This group is highly heterogeneous, including people from all social classes, from the country gentry, provincial businessmen who see being in the C. of E. as a step up from the Free Churches, to working-class people who also see being C. of E. as an important component of being respectable.[15] The active laity may be motivated by other theological beliefs, particularly likely among the more Catholic Anglicans, or by political ideas that the Church should be more radical in its commitments, which it cannot be in the present situation, or by a mixture of the two (see Valerie Pitt's Memorandum of Dissent to the 1970 Report).[16] For some, the Church of England is a Christian religious body which ought to be separate from the State, at least in part, so that it can run its own religious affairs, and in part so that it can be more critical of the State when necessary.

> I want to see the Church free to be herself; and she is not free if she cannot appoint her own bishops, and reform her own liturgy, and if she is at the mercy of a Parliament which is non-Anglican and non-Christian. (Trevor Huddleston, Bishop of Stepney, 29 March 1970)[17]

One of the most important ritual events for many people in modern Britain is *Remembrance Day*. This is a complex ritual event involving the Church of England in its role as the national Church, the British Legion, the local community, and, at the national level, the monarch. The ritual is both an important national event in which the dead soldiers of two world wars are remembered, and an important local event involving people from local areas in ritual action too. Every local community, in the case of England every parish, has a special place where the poppy wreath is laid. This may be in the church itself, or by a stone pillar outside the church. In either case this place is regarded, certainly by most of the older generation, as a set-apart, sacred place, just as Poppy Day and Remembrance Sunday is a sacred time. Lloyd Warner, writing about American Memorial Day ceremonies, sees such an event as a cult of the dead. It has the important characteristic of uniting people of a variety of religious beliefs and of none, in one ritual action.

> It dramatically expresses the sentiments of unity of all the living among themselves, of all the living to all the dead, and of all the living and dead as a group to the gods. The gods—Catholic, Protestant and Jewish—lose their sectarian definitions,

limitations, and foreignness among themselves and become objects of worship for the whole group and the protectors of everyone . . . Each ritual also stressed the fact that the war was an experience where everyone sacrificed and some died, not as members of a separate group, but as citizens of a whole community.[18]

In England there is more sense of belonging to one nation historically than in America, but still the ritual of Remembrance Day serves to unite people of many different denominations, and of none, in one ritual. In many towns and villages of England the ritual consists of a processional march by members of the local British Legion, an ex-servicemen's organisation, to the local Church of England for a service of remembrance, which includes prayers and hymns of an inter-denominational type, and the laying of the poppy wreath near the sacred stone which will have some, or all, of the names of the dead from that parish in the world wars engraved on it. This ritual shows the Church of England as a national Church. The ritual is one which has elements of both civic and religious ritual, as defined in previous chapters, present in it. It is civic ritual because the local community, or the nation state is the limit of concern for most people; it is not a universal ritual, it is not oriented to all human beings killed in wars. It is for the dead of a specific area, and of a particular nation state in two wars. Yet it is also a religious ritual in that it is intended by most of the participants to relate to God. It is a mixed ritual in that for many of the participants the civic aspect is the most important. Yet by being focused on the dead, it carries potentially a high element of 'numinous' experience.

It seemed that out of battle I escaped
Down some profound dull tunnel, long since scooped
Through granites which titanic wars had groined.
Yet also there encumbered sleepers groaned,
Too fast in thought or death to be bestirred.
Then, as I probed them, one sprang up, and stared
With piteous recognition in fixed eyes.
Lifting distressful hands as if to bless.

And no guns thumped, or down the flues made moan.
'Strange friend', I said 'here is no cause to mourn'.

Wilfred Owen[19]

The Church of England also appears as a national Church and provider of civic ritual, with a religious element, on the occasion of life-cycle rituals of members of the Royal Family, especially weddings and funerals, and funerals of national heroes such as Winston Churchill. These ritual occasions make use of Westminster Abbey or St Paul's Cathedral, and their Anglican staff. The Church of England is used as a provider of nationalist ritual on these special occasions. The ritual events of the Royal Family are part of the English system of nationalist rituals, in that their essential reference is to the position of the Royal Family as the pinnacle of the Society's hierarchy.

New forms of civic ritual are continually emerging in modern Britain, and as these take over successfully from the civic ritual of the Church of England, a greater degree of separation between religious and civic ritual becomes possible. It is worth looking at some examples of the new forms of civic ritual which have developed at the level of the nation state and local community. Other forms of civic ritual will be examined in the chapter on life-cycle rituals.

The most important development has probably been that of radio and, since the 1950s, television. Many people now watch a ritual event on television, whereas before its existence they may have attended a church service. The Coronation of Queen Elizabeth is the most important example, although even then, in 1953, a large number attended church services on Coronation Day—a major example of the mixture of civic and religious ritual in the Church of England. There will probably be less people in the churches at the next Coronation, although this is difficult to know for there are no accurate figures for the last Coronation Day services. Other civic ritual events get large television audiences, and thereby provide civic ritual events in the home, and so people feel less need to go to a church service or its equivalent. For instance, the main Remembrance Day ritual from the Cenotaph is televised, thereby reducing the numbers who go to the local ritual in their parish church (quite apart from the changing generational structures; i.e. as the years go by, less and less people remember the wars, for they were either not born then, or too young to remember).

Events like the Last Night of the Proms are also part of the increasing exposure of the population to nationalist events which television has brought. The songs which are sung at this particular event, and those at the Wembley Cup Final, have an overtone of religiosity, in that 'God' may be mentioned in the verses, and the tunes have a sacred character about them, often being hymn tunes in any case. Examples are: 'O God our help in ages past'; Parry's setting of Jerusalem—'And did those feet in ancient times, walk upon England's pastures green'; Elgar's 'Land of Hope and Glory'; and of course the National Anthem—'God Save the Queen'. The act of watching these events on television, with the family and sometimes friends, does have some real effect on people, and the fact that there is a national broadcasting system in Britain, the BBC, serves these nationalist civic ritual events especially well.

Apart from this type of use of television, there is a separate use of the medium, which can also exist in the cinema, and that is to portray historical–mythic events and figures in dramatic terms, around nationalist themes. Britain seems to excel itself in the production of this type of film and television presentation in a way that few other countries do. (The American western is perhaps an exception here, but the western does not contain quite the same kind of mythic event as the historical dramas about Britain.) There are numerous examples. On television there has been 'The Six Wives of Henry VIII' and 'Elizabeth R', which portrayed the founding figures of the modern English nation state. In 1972 there was a thirteen-part serial called 'The British Empire', which caused controversy at the time because it failed in some people's eyes to portray the Empire story in a sufficiently mythic way. The faults here were mainly ones of production; the series was not produced with the same dramatic quality and professional finish as BBC audiences had come to expect. In the cinema, the late sixties and early seventies saw *Waterloo*, *The Battle of Britain*, *Mary, Queen of Scots*, *Anne of a*

8 The Queen before the robing and crowning in the coronation,
June 1953.

9 Remembrance Day.
Queen lays a wreath of po
at the Cenotaph, Whit
London. Note the presen
clergy and bishops at
national ritual.

10. The funeral of Wi
Churchill in St Paul's C
dral, London, 1965. (Us
Church of England cath
for a ritual of the nation-s

Thousand Days, and *Henry VIII*. Some of these were given a 'Royal Performance', with either the Queen or the Queen Mother being present. This gives these films added publicity and charisma.

These forms of film and television drama are, then, forms of civic ritual. People watching them are involved in a process similar to listening to a myth being told in a non-industrial society, or seeing a myth of the origins of the tribe being enacted in a dramatic form in such societies. Mircea Eliade writes

> . . . a myth is the true history of what came to pass at the beginning of Time, and which provides the pattern for human behaviour. In imitating the exemplary acts of a god or of a mythic hero, or simply by recounting their adventures, the man of an archaic society detaches himself from profane time and magically re-enters the Great Time, the Sacred Time.[20]

Modern man uses electrical media of all types to alter his experience of time, to avoid boredom, to have a 'good time'. He seeks to be transported from the everyday world and ordinary time into a set-apart time, 'entertainment' time. When people watch films and television of the type instanced above they may see themselves as seeking 'entertainment', which here means a way of altering their experince of time in a magical way—to see people who are dead, reliving their lives in 120 minutes. Cinema and television are really magical; just as the theatre can be.

Sports also carry some nationalistic civic ritual, as well as local civic ritual, around the town or city area's football team, for example. Soccer now involves whole nations in a world-wide competition, second only to the Olympic Games in the amount of ritual action surrounding the national teams. Supporters of teams wear special articles of clothing, sing special songs, wear special emblems, and perform special actions in support of their teams, and to help them win. The amount of nationalist commitment has been heightened by the coming of television for it shows the 'home' audience the national team, wherever it may be, performing on behalf of the nation itself. The commentaries emphasise the nationalist element by concentrating

H

heavily on their nation's team, and by being euphoric when the team scores a goal, or wins a medal, or wins a game. The audience watching at home becomes involved in the sporting events very largely on the basis of national feeling in the case of nearly all international events. It is difficult to know empirically whether the nationalism is there to be tapped, as it were, by these events, or whether the events themselves, and the televising of them to millions of people, itself increases nationalist feelings among the population. As long as these sporting events are surrounded in this way with nationalism, so long will the events be in part civic ritual for the modern nation state.

At a local level too, teams, especially soccer teams and cricket teams in England, are surrounded by ritual action of the local civic group. It is rare to find a person who lives in a city such as Leeds, supporting a football team from the Midlands. Support is given to the local team of the town because it represents the local group; it would be seen as disloyal for a person born and bred in a particular town to support a team from another town.

The existence of these new forms of national civic ritual lessens the demands made on the Church of England for such civic ritual, and thus the Church is becoming a more specifically 'religious' ritual organisation than it was, even before the Second World War.

THE FEAST OF CHRISTMAS

This is a very complex ritual event for it involves many different types of ritual action. It is a key festival of the Christian religious year; a family ritual; a ritual of gift exchange; a ritual of Mammon; and a ritual of the Winter Solstice. In modern Europe and North America it is not, for most people, primarily an event in the Christian year, although the Christian aspect is certainly present, and an essential one at that. Christmas expresses a residual Christianity. It is a civic ritual of the family, crucially involving gift exchange and the sending of cards to friends to keep up a social bond. Commercial capitalism has developed the gift exchange aspect in the last few decades to a very great extent, but the ritual of gift exchange is to some extent independent of this. During the Second World War in Britain, the gifts were still exchanged, even though commerce and advertising were at a very low level of activity at this period. There is now a complex interplay of the family gift exchange ritual, and the interests of commercial groups in persuading people to spend more money than usual at Christmas.

It is possible to see what gift exchange and card sending express by examining the process whereby gift exchange and card sending *cease* between two people or two familes. Two families of orientation are joined by a marriage of a husband and wife, and this sets up a social relationship which often exists primarily through the exchange of cards and sometimes gifts, especially at Christmas, which is even more crucial than birthdays. If later this couple become divorced, the card and gift exchange tends to stop between the parents-in-law, and the son- or daughter-in-law, and also between the two families of orientation. Whether to send a card to the ex-wife or ex-husband also becomes problematic for the other partner. The problem centres around the fact that card sending and gift exchange imply that an important social bond, which both parties hold, in some degree, to be a desirable relationship, is broken ritually by divorce court proceedings. Thus gift exchange and card sending contradict the nature of a divorce, which is a ritualised way of breaking a social relationship.

People who live long distances away from one another, or who do not often meet, and yet still hold some degree of social relationship to be desirable, will exchange cards, if not gifts. This is a key way of maintaining the relationship. People may complain about the number of cards they are involved in sending to friends of the family at Christmas, but they can also be very concerned when someone who normally has sent a Christmas card every year, one year does not send one. This can cause hurt, even though almost nothing else exists by way of a relationship between the people concerned.

Christmas parties are another important aspect of the ritual season, for a loosening of the usual normative controls over action is socially licensed at this time. Work, for instance, is allowed to become less central to people, even before the full holiday starts; this is especially true on the day of the office party, or the day after a party, such as the ones on New Year's Eve. People who usually keep body contact to a minimum, for example a young female secretary and her boss, may kiss under the mistletoe at a party. The use of alcohol enables people to interact more directly than is usually allowed, and serves to create an atmosphere of 'good will'. This proves difficult to establish in many organisations because of the usually high degree of formality and lack of emotional expression between the different ranks of a hierarchy, yet some office parties approach this by allowing the high ranks to engage in behaviour which is normally unacceptable. Once the high-ranking people have played a party game and adopted postures or made expressions which could normally be defined as undignified, then the party can 'swing'. If those of high rank do not, early on, engage in such behaviour, then the party will tend to remain stilted, because those lower down the hierarchy do not want to step too far out of line in front of their superiors who, by not joining in party games, are not licensing others to be too boisterous.[21]

In manual, working-class situations, such as factories and building sites, mines, and railways, the management rarely join in 'celebrations' with the workers for the class differences are too strong to allow for this, even at Christmas. Only in smaller, paternalistic, work situations could this occur, and even then the interaction is likely to be limited to a Christmas drink, on the middle classes' terms—sherry not beer.

Christmas cannot overcome basic class conflict between working-class people, and middle-class people. The office party is possible for the clerks and secretaries share a similar life-style sufficiently to allow for some meeting. They share some consensus about the hierarchic structure of their work situation which allows a loosening under special ritualised settings. Where such a degree of consensus is lacking, as it often is between managers and manual workers, then there can be no ritualised loosening of the norms, in any case, at work, or outside the work setting. There can be no loosening even in a ritual setting of what is not there in any case.

Parties involve drinking and some eating together. Christmas

Day is marked by special food, and a special meal in England—the Christmas dinner. It is the eating of a special meal together which is a high point of this civic ritual of the family. Many families of procreation invite the grandparents to share this meal; or one grandparent couple one year and the other the following year. The family is ritually unified over three generations by the eating of this meal. It is a communion meal, but without sacrifice.[22]

Christmas Trees and Lights
The ritual symbolism of the tree with lights on it is North European and pre-Christian in origin. Indeed the first Christian missionaries used a date already sacred in the calendar, in late December, for their own feast of the Incarnation. The ancient part of this festival of the Winter Solstice is still with us, partly because in Europe winter is dark and dead, the trees are bare, the ground is infertile. The evergreen tree is a symbol of fertility, and the lights symbolic of regeneration. The tree with lights on it is a symbol of hope; hope for the sun to return, for the ground and the trees to become fertile again. This symbolism is found in many cultures—the tree as a basic phallic symbol; fire and the sun are also phallic symbols, bearing promise of renewal, fertility and light. Even modern man, in European and North American cities, is still aware of the change in nature at this time of the year—the cold, the darkness, the black, leafless trees in the streets and parks. Modern urban man needs a symbol of hope in the depths of winter, which even electric lights on artificial trees can provide. Life is so much the richer for people through the survival of this ritual symbolism.

Many people who have spent Christmas away from the European cultural and geographical region, but were reared in it as children, feel a sense of its importance for them when they see a Christmas tree again for the first time. Mircea Eliade has written: '. . . in mythologies and religions, the principal meanings of the Tree-symbolism—otherwise complex enough—are bound up with the ideas of periodic and unending renewal, or regeneration, of "the source of life and youth", of immortality and of absolute reality.'[23]

Chapter Six

Life-cycle Rituals

INTRODUCTION

Life-cycle rituals are key points at which culture and social structure interrelate with the biological growth and decay of human bodies. There are always two sets of problems with which life-cycle rituals have to deal; those concerned with the life of the group and those concerned with the feelings aroused in people by biological processes. For example, rituals around childbirth involve the group accepting the child, a new member, into its patterns and way of life; and they deal with the feelings of the mother and father by publicly articulating some sense of awe, and thanks for the birth of their baby. Similarly, with the death of someone, the group which has lost a member can use ritual to reintegrate itself. The family, or the community, or a whole nation, affirms its continued existence through its collective ritual action. Ritual concerned with burial of the dead also may cope with the feelings of grief and loss, and aid mourning, for those people who were particularly close to the deceased.

Marriage ceremonies too are concerned with both areas; the two families involved meet and affirm a new social connection between them as a result of the marriage of one family's son to another family's daughter. There is also implicitly some recognition that the children from the marriage will be regarded as legitimate heirs eventually. The wedding also sanctions sexuality and the sexual feelings of the couple; and this is particularly true in modern marriages based on choice of the partner by the couple themselves, as a result of 'falling in love'.

Life-cycle rituals are of critical importance for understanding the ways a modern industrial society relates, or fails to relate, to the human body. Sexuality and birth, illness and death, these are the central biological processes involved in such rituals. The rituals can either aid people relate to their bodies and their biology, or they can block off awareness of the body, and provide ways of 'spiritualising' the body's feelings. Which of these life-cycle rituals 'ought' to do depends on basic views about the nature of man; for those who believe man is a spiritual being the type of rituals which spiritualise the experience will obviously be preferable. The view to be taken here is that man is primarily a bodily organism, although of a unique kind.

Any analysis, whether it be social, scientific or philosophical, ought to start with this fact, because we do know it to be true, at least as far as it goes. We can never know whether man is a spirit who has ended up on the earth, but will return to his spiritual existence after he dies, in the same sense of 'know'. At least, not this side of the grave. So it seems best to start with what we do have and do know, that is that man is *at least* a *bodily* being.

However, this does not fully deal with the problem raised above, for even though the analysis begins on the assumption that man is a body, it does not follow that rituals which spiritualise this bodily experience are necessarily a 'bad thing'. Yet if the sociology, psychology, and social anthropology of ritual are not to be drearily neutral, some implicit judgement on this issue must be made. The view to be taken here is that in so far as rituals focus attention on another, so-called spiritual, realm, to the exclusion of this bodily one, they are to be criticised. This is a view which is held by an increasing number of Christians, who see that many ways of understanding Christianity have been based on a dualism deriving from ancient Greek philosophy, and from Manichean beliefs, and are not sufficiently Hebraic and Biblical. They would claim Christianity is not basically dualistic, neither anti-matter nor anti-body, in the way it has often been presented in its historical forms. The central doctrine of the incarnation implies that matter and the body are capable of fulfilment through 'grace'.[1] Note, for instance, 'Thy Kingdom come, on earth as it is in Heaven'—heaven may not mean a spiritual realm, akin to the life outside Plato's cave, but something more like 'as it is in man's best thoughts for his future'.

The way it is proposed to examine rituals here is not, then, anti-religious or anti-Christian, given what has just been said. Behind all views lies an assumption that there is *some* truth-state about man's nature, which philosophy, biology, anthropology, sociology, psychology, all seek by using rational and empirical methods, and that this 'truth' cannot be conceptually different from the notion of 'truth' which world religions have sought after. Perhaps religions should leave this matter now to 'philosophical anthropology' and its rational methods, and concentrate on aiding men to live in a state of less than perfect knowledge about this critically important issue.

INITIATION INTO SEX-ROLES

In Western industrial societies there is a central social role differentiation made on the basis of biological sexual characteristics, those of 'men' and 'women'. These roles have to be learnt, and such learning may take many forms, for different aspects of the sex roles require different types of learning. For example, sexual intercourse is in large part a matter of physical or physiological learning; the emotional relationship in which intercourse takes place requires learning about feelings between people; being a husband or wife, father or mother, requires learning of socio-cultural roles.[2] The central interest of this section is in the part certain kinds of ritual action play in the learning and, more crucially, identification with, the sexual roles of the society.

In simpler, less industrial societies, there are often rituals which aid in this process of identification with sexual roles, and many of these have been studied and analysed by anthropologists and some psychologists. They tend to occur at the time of puberty and there are examples of both initiation rites at this time for both boys and girls.[3] The process may last years, or a few weeks, and often involves ordeals producing fear and suffering in the young males.[4] They compel the young person, as Mircea Eliade writes, 'to assume a new mode of being, that which is proper to an adult—namely, that which is conditioned by the almost simultaneous revelation of the sacred, of death and of sexuality.'[5]

There are no such clearly marked rituals in modern industrial society, but there are many pieces of ritual action which clearly do have a similar part to play. Children's games at birthday parties and Christmas parties, as well as in less adult-controlled games played on the streets by children whose parents allow such street play, as most of the working class do, or games in school playgrounds, often serve to teach sex roles and instil some degree of identification with them. Sports have a key role here too—boys play football, girls do not, typically. Fighting is for boys.[6] Cricket is largely a male game, but tennis, hockey, swimming and athletics are mixed sexually.

The pattern seems to be that although there are some games still which are very largely male dominated games, there are mixed sports, but none exclusively for females. There are some activities which are more female dominated outside sport, but they are domestic, or linked with learning domestic work, including child rearing. (Skipping is for girls, and only very young boys. This seems not to reflect anything intrinsic in the action, so is it purely accidental that it has been seen as for girls in English culture, the key point being that something is reserved for girls alone?)

Central to the male identification in Western culture is the ability to fight; for schoolboys of all classes the fighter is a central figure; the one who can use his fists or wrestle and win is considered the best one to know in a school. In teenage gangs of males the fighter, who may by this age use weapons such as a knife, is also a key figure; and such gangs may well develop some 'hazing' rite which all members are put through, either on joining the group or at some other point in the life of the gang.[7] In society as a whole, the soldier is a highly esteemed figure by nearly all sections of the society, and until recently the conscientious objector was considered a coward—a very negative term for a male who, because he will not fight, is seen as not fully masculine by most other men and women. Only among the youth group which has protested against Vietnam has this pattern altered in any significant way. The ritual celebration of the masculine 'fighter' hero-figure occurs in numerous films, TV serials, 'Welcome Homes' of soldiers, boxing, and some pop songs.

The film *King and Country* is significant as an exploration of this theme of the male who does not want to fight—but it is an atypical film for the period 1950-65. The huge success for the James Bond films shows the extent to which this figure is still seen as some kind of hero-figure, compared with the young man in *King and Country*.[8] Bond is a figure who carried the masculine ability to fight, to be able to 'take care of himself', to an extreme, but because this trait it still highly esteemed in the culture of Britain and America, at least for males, he is highly popular among all major groups, with the possible exception of the liberal professions.

Such masculine ideals are found in modern industrial societies in the twentieth century as a result of the wars in the first half of the century, and ever-ready attitude to fight if attacked, held during the fifties and sixties in West and East European societies.[9] The world wars affected the socialisation of every generation of males since 1910, either quite directly, in that young males were needed by the armed forces of the major powers who were willing to see fighting as a highly esteemed activity, or the effects were indirect, in that fathers reared under these conditions came to see masculinity in these terms, and so transmitted such a notion of masculinity to their sons, even up to the present day. Males who were between 15 and 25 in 1940 were between 45 and 55 in 1970, that is at the height of their social influence. The sons of their sons are now being socialised and it is too early to see how masculinity will be understood—given no international war. Will young men reared under peacetime affluent conditions in Western Europe, or North America, be prepared to fight? Against Russians and East Europeans? Chinese? Others in their own society? These are not perceived as enemies at the moment, in the way Germany was in the past, for they do not attack. Even with modern nuclear weapons some personnel are still needed from the ordinary population to fight, and it is choosing this group which may be problematic in the future.

Given this wider historical, societal context, the role that ritual action plays can be better understood, for it may either aid identification with the fighting male, or for some groups enable them to develop alternative masculine identities, e.g. the sports star, or the pop star.[10] Similarly, there are ritual aspects to dress and the parading of it at parties, or in the street, or in the cinemas and dance halls, for the clothes men and women wear on these occasions are not utilitarian uniforms, of the type worn for work. They are expressive of a sensual and aesthetic approach to the world which is now widespread among the affluent population of industrial societies, no longer restricted to the upper classes. Since 1960 there has been a major change in respect to males' clothes and appearance. Young males now wear 'costume'—ritual attire.[11]

CHANGES IN ENGLISH LIFE-CYCLE RITUALS

Every human society has some ritual surrounding transitions of social position connected with the human biological life cycle. These are termed here life-cycle rituals. They are a sub-set of the set of rituals which might be termed *rites de passage*, following van Gennep.[12] Others are concerned with crises in life, such as ill-health, both mental and physical, accidents, or rituals to prevent such occurrences. A third distinct sub-set of natural-cycle rituals are concerned with season events, such as spring, harvest, the winter and summer solstices, the beginning of a new year. Another sub-set are concerned with changes in social position not concerned with the life cycle, except incidentally; these are particularly important in changes in positions of authority and power.[13]

All rites of passage have a common structure according to van Gennep. First, there is the stage of 'separation' from the old order of things or previous social condition; second, a 'marginal, transition' period which is described as a 'liminal' phase, a sacred period between the two other stages; third, there is the stage of 'incorporation' or aggregation into a new condition or social situation. The *rites de passage* in tribal societies tend to enact death to one condition and resurrection to another condition.[14] There is a sense in which this is a definition of *rites de passage*, that is rituals which have these three stages are called *'rites de passage'* by van Gennep.

In modern industrial society many of the rituals associated with the life cycle are still based on the social relations of the family and kinship groups involved. In this way they are similar to the rituals of the life cycle in less industrial and less differentiated societies. Max Gluckman makes an important distinction between *'ritualisation of social relations'* where the persons related in various ways to the central participants as well as these themselves, perform prescribed actions according to their secular roles; and *'ritualism'* in which the ritual actions are related to mystical notions, 'but which do not develop the ritualism out of the roles and relationships of the whole congregation involved'.[15] The life-cycle rituals in England are a mixture of these two analytical types, and the recent changes which have been introduced and the reports on these rituals are concerned with the problems which derive from the mixture. Basically the problems stem from the fact that the rituals are used by many English people as rites of passage within or between families. They are in this way an example of 'ritualisation of social relations'. At the same time they are religious rituals, first and foremost, for the full-time clergy, and highly committed laity—Gluckman's 'ritualism'. They are rites of initiation into the Church or sacraments of grace, as in the case of marriage, which are ambiguously related to the English population. The Church of England is, as was shown in the chapter on civic and nationalist rituals, a religious group, membership of which many English people see as part of being 'English'. For others, the 'Anglicans', it is one among many of the possible ways of being a Christian, not of being English. Some clergy and laity ask why the Church should baptise, marry, or even bury, people who are not committed Christians, but want to use the life-cycle rituals of the English Church as part of what might be called 'folk' religion. The difficulty here is that the ordinary people regard themselves as Christian, but the 'Anglicans', both clergy and laity, see them as only half-hearted Christians, and not very highly committed to the

Church of England as a religious institution, concerned with the preaching of the gospel and the dispensation of sacramental grace.

The Church of England is an *Ecclesia* type of religious organisation. 'Members are *born into* the ecclesia; they do not have to join it' (Yinger quoting Becker).[16] Yet many of its members who are most active in its organisational life think that people should become members of the Church more through consciously joining it as an organisation. This would make it more like a 'denomination' in this respect.[17] Yet historically and structurally, for many English people, the Church of England is not just one more denomination, it is the Church of the nation, i.e. an Ecclesia (in sociological terms that is). The tensions arise particularly in the ritual of baptism, less so in confirmation, and to some extent in regard to marriage. Funerals are less problematic, for few clergy or laity would want to refuse a funeral service to anyone who asked.

There is a problem with the sociological use of the term 'ecclesia', however, which is that it is very near the exact opposite of part of its original, theological meaning. 'Ecclesia' is in origin an Old Testament idea, and means those who have been 'called out', separated from the ordinary.[18] This is not the same idea as that of a national, established Church, into which all who are born in a particular nation are, *ipso facto*, members of that Church, either by compulsion, or by some kind of choice. Part of the original meaning of 'ecclesia' is perhaps closer to what sociologists call 'sect' than to an established Church. It therefore aids communication between sociologists and clergy, theologians, and laity, if the term *'Established Church'* is used for a church such as the Church of England. *'Denomination'* would be used for the Anglican Church in those societies where it is not 'established' by law.[19] There are some areas in modern Anglicanism where it is less of an established Church, by not supporting the ruling class groups in society, for example in South Africa, or to a lesser extent Southern Rhodesia, and even modern England. It thus has some of the characteristics of a 'denomination' in that it has more tension between its values and those of the ruling classes in these white, capitalist societies than would a fully 'Established Church' type of religious organisation.

To return to the rituals in the early part of the life cycle. In a society like that of England in the twentieth century, there is confusion about the use of the established Church's rituals in relation to the events of the life cycle. This affects the following rites concerned with birth and growth to maturity: baptism, thanksgiving after childbirth (called by most people 'churching' of women), confirmation and first communion. During the 1960s there was a sharp decline in the statistics for baptisms and confirmations. There are no official statistics for the number of 'churchings', but general impressions among the clergy are that this too has declined. In the early 1970s well over 45 per cent of the English population used baptism.

Clergy in some parishes have felt that they did not want to baptise in an indiscriminate manner all who came to ask for their children 'to be done', regardless of the degree of connection between a family and the Church of England. Some clergy have introduced services which bless the new-born baby, and give thanks for the new birth, but stop short of baptism, which they regard as a central sacrament of the Church, the main way of being initiated into the Church. Unless parents are seriously intending to teach their young children about Christianity, these clergy feel it is wrong to baptise newly born babies just because they were born in England. It is not possible to estimate how far this view of baptism on the part of some of the parish clergy influences the overall statistics, but it must play some part. It does, however, show that these clergy perceive modern England as, in large part, a non-Christian society.

A report on the rites of initiation in the Church of England, published in 1971, marked an important stage in the debate within the Church of England about baptism and confirmation.[20] The report said that there should be a clear differentiation between a service of thanksgiving for the birth of a child, and baptism, which should be *the* rite of initiation into the Christian Church. It makes the point that 'naming' is a civil act performed at the registrar's office, and nothing to do with the Church's rites. The priest uses the name of the child in both the service of thanksgiving and in baptism, and brings the child's name into contact with God.[21] There are at this point major discrepancies between the way many ordinary English people perceive what they call 'christening', and the way clergy, and élite laity, perceive services of thanksgiving and baptism. The Church's rites are embedded in a socio-cultural context in which meanings are transmitted from one generation to the next by actions and feelings, rather than by what Basil Berstein calls *elaborated codes* or, in his earlier formulation, 'formal language' of the type used by the middle classes.[22] The report on Christian initiation takes almost no account of these problems. It seeks a tidy administrative and theological solution to the issues raised by the present situation, rather than basing its recommendations on any carefully researched understanding of the complex meanings people give to these life-cycle rituals.

One of the most important consequences of making baptism *the* rite of Christian initiation is that the place of confirmation becomes problematic in the scheme. The report recommends that confirmation should be seen as a service of commitment by the person being confirmed to the Christian faith, and a commissioning by the bishop or his deputy 'of the fully in-structed and responsible Christian adult for the work of ministry and mission in the world to which he is thereby committing himself'.[23] This means a change from seeing confirmation as a necessary rite, after baptism, before the person is ready for his first communion. This is how confirma-tion has been seen, and still is by very many laity and clergy. In the past a person wishing to join the Church of England from another major denomination, who had already been baptised, would be required to prepare and then be confirmed by a bishop. The report recommends, consistently, that such people should in future only be required to have instruction from a priest before they take communion in the Church of England. This is consistent with the report's view of these matters, but what of the 'convert' who would like some ritual event to mark his entry into a new Church, and not just some instruction from a priest, usually in the priest's private study? Confirmation once acted as a rite of passage from one Church to another, which many felt was necessary, otherwise they may as well stay in the Church they originally belonged to. It might well be that because there is a felt need by some converts for a rite of passage, a modified version of confirmation will continue to be used, in spite of the attempt to tidy matters up on the part of the Commission on Christian Initiation, which produced the above-mentioned report. The strains between the Church of England's various commissions and synods, and the majority of English people who quietly persist, in their untidy ways, to regard the C. of E. as their Church when they need it, will continue, and deepen with each attempt to find neat solutions.

A number of new ritual acts are also being recommended for introduction into the baptism service. The central ritual act has always been the use of water, and the saying of the words 'I baptise you in the name of the Father and of the Son and of the Holy Ghost. Amen.' There follows, usually, the signing with the cross in which the priest makes the sign of the cross on the person's forehead. A new element in use in some churches is the giving of a lighted candle to the family, as a symbol of the light of Christ to guide the child.

The parents should keep the candle carefully and use it at important events in the child's life. It could, for example, be the central candle at birthday parties. As a child grows up it will be a constant reminder of the significance of his baptism, and it will give his parents an opportunity to explain to him something of what happened when he was baptised.'[24]

All these ritual acts are performed during the central stage of the rite as a whole. They occur in the *liminal stage*, the most sacred of any rite of passage.[25] Firstly, the godparents on behalf of the baby, or in the case of an adult, the person himself, are separated from the past state. In the case of Christian baptism, this is a state of original sin, a state of life outside that of the Christian fold. So this section consists of asking if the person repents of his sins, renounces evil, and turns to Christ. The person having said he does turn to Christ and renounces evil, and repents, is ritually ready for the next stage of the rite, his baptism. The major element in the ritual is water, and this has

Press Association

11   Local civic ritual. Supporters of Arsenal welcome home their team
and the F.A. cup they have won, 1971.

12   Christmas tree, Trafalgar Square, London. The tree has been
given by the people of Oslo, Norway, every year since the Second
World War. Carols are sung and there is dancing as the lights are
switched on.

Press Association

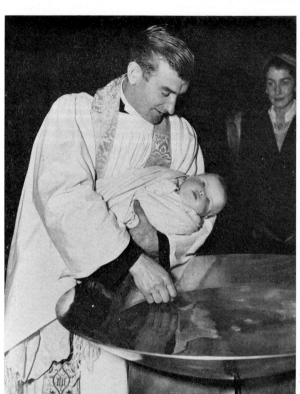

13 Baptism. Water is ess[e] in this initiation ritual, used life-cycle ritual by over hal[f] English population.

Press Association

14 Marriage. 'Those whom hath joined together let no put asunder.'

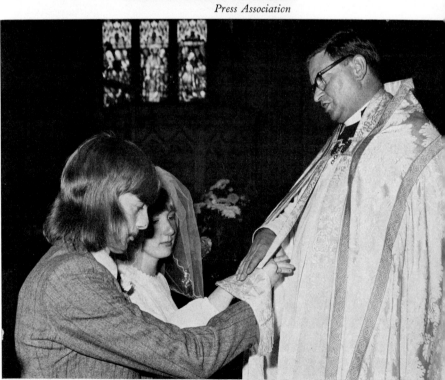

Photograph by J.

Press Association

15   Burial. A whole local community attending the burial of two children in consecrated ground.

16   A dance—a place for meeting possible marital partners. This picture shows a revival of rock 'n roll at Wembley in 1972.

Press Association

17   Football. A game which aids male identification for boys. Some
footballers become famous figures in the whole country, like George
Best in the picture above, 1972.

to be blessed before it can be used for the sacred act itself. 'Bless, we pray thee, this water, that all who are baptised in it may be *born again* in Christ; that being baptised into his Death, and receiving forgiveness of all their sins, they may know the power of his resurrection, and may walk in *newness of life . . .*' (author's italics). The priest will make the sign of the cross with his outstretched hands over the water in the font. Water is being used as a symbol of death and resurrection, death to one state of life and being born again into another, in this case as a member of the Christian Church. Water in human life does have both the capacity to kill—storms at sea, floods—and is also essential to growth and fertility, to life itself. This symbolic value is explained in many Church pamphlets on the subject.[26]

The person and the water have both been prepared for the liminal stage, where the sacred act takes place, as mentioned above. There then follows the third stage of incorporation into the new social group, in this case the Church. The priest says 'God has received you by Baptism into his Church. We therefore welcome you into the Lord's family, as fellow members of the Body of Christ, as children of the same heavenly Father, as inheritors with us of the Kingdom of God.' In order to make this more clear to the relatives there is an increasing tendency to try to have the baptism ritual within the context of the main Sunday service of worship, the Eucharist, or Family Communion. This makes it clearer that the child, or baptised person, is being incorporated into the Church as a body of people, whereas the ritual, when performed separately as is still often the case, and until the sixties nearly always was, appears more as a private ritual for the family as a group.[27]

The Christian Initiation Report recommended the introduction of yet another ritual act during the liminal stage, which follows from their view that confirmation is not a necessary sacrament before a person can receive Holy Communion, and this is the use of anointing with holy oil, and the laying on of hands. 'Anointing with oil which is specially consecrated for the purpose and symbolises messianic anointing by the Spirit of God has been a familiar accessory to Baptism.'[28] The familiarity

I

is obviously not found among most English people; the Commission mean familiar in the Christian Church elsewhere, and in other times. Their reason for putting it with baptism itself is that it makes it clear to all concerned that no extra rite or sacrament is needed other than baptism, using the name of the Trinity, and water, for being made a member of the Christian Church. The anointing with oil and laying on of hands, if done in a confirmation ritual, seems to imply that they are necessary before someone can receive Holy Communion. But this is not the case in any Christian theology, though it has grown to seem so in the Church of England over the years.[29] Anointing with oil, giving a lighted candle, laying on of hands, are optional extras in the ritual of baptism; the lighted candle ritual is built into the New Series II baptism service. The others occur in 'high', Catholic-oriented Churches. Baptism is recognised by the Church of England as a sacrament which can be administered by any Christian, and certainly by any Christian minister of any Church who uses the Trinitarian formula, and water (this would exclude, for example, Unitarians, who would not use the Trinitarian formula; and it would exclude Humanist rites of initiation).

Confirmation in the Church of England usually occurs at the age of fourteen to eighteen years. This is later than in the Roman Catholic Church, where it tends to be at the age of seven or eight years. In the Free Churches the age at which people take on full membership tends to be later. The rite of confirmation still continues, although the numbers being confirmed, as a proportion of their age group, has fallen.

Before being confirmed, young people and adults must undergo preparation by a priest. This will usually take the form of a series of meetings with a group of confirmation candidates, sexually mixed but of the same age-grade, conducted by the priest. There may be twelve, or as many as twenty, such meetings, held once a week. The candidates must know the Lord's Prayer, the Ten Commandments, and the Creed. Classes will involve candidates learning the meaning of these, as well as something about the sacramental life of the Church.

Many young people who are confirmed later drop out of

regular church attendance, and often feel that 'nothing happened' when they were confirmed. The rite does not live up to the expectations they have of it. Perhaps for this reason the Church thought it necessary to reconsider the best age for adult commitment to the Church, and seems to favour a later age for this type of commitment.[30]

MARRIAGE AND SEXUALITY

Marriage is still a crucial ritual event for many who marry in the Church of England. The numbers who do so has fallen during this century. About 45 per cent of marriages in 1967 took place in Church of England churches in England and Wales. About 35 per cent are civil ceremonies.[31] Marriage is a ritual event which many still assume the Church of England will provide for them even if they are not regular church-goers. It is part of the function of a nationally established Church to do this in the eyes of many English people. For some clergy the same problem arises for marriage as for baptism. Should non-church attenders be married in church? What do the vows which the bride and groom take mean to them in a society in which divorce is on the increase? There were 28,542 petitions for divorce in 1962; 55,007 in 1968. There is considerable confusion here between the way the committed Anglicans, obviously including most clergy, see the role of marriage as a Christian sacrament, and involving a relationship between two people, and God, in such a way that it cannot be broken, and the recognitition by the State that divorce is possible after the irretrievable breakdown of a marriage. The sole grounds for divorce introduced in 1969 after a report by the Church of England, published in 1966, called 'Putting Asunder', allowed this for the citizen, although seeing the committed Christian as accepting voluntarily more discipline than this. The confusion still reigns at the time of writing (1972) in that the Church of England has not decided yet to remarry in a church rite people who have been divorced and whose spouses are still alive. There has been considerable shift in opinion on this issue in the early 1970s. In 1895 the Lambeth Conference of Anglican Bishops throughout the world held that no 'guilty' or 'innocent' divorced person could marry again in church. This was reiterated in 1908 and 1930. In 1938 the Convocations of Canterbury and York resolved that the marriage service should not be used in the case of anyone with the former partner still living. In 1957 this resolution formed part of a statement declared to be an Act of the Canterbury Convocation. The Report of the 1971 Church of England Commission on Marriage, Divorce and the Church was very different.

> Is there . . . a growing consensus that such persons [i.e. divorced people wishing to remarry in church] with due safeguards, may properly have their marriages solemnised according the rites of the church? . . . It is possible that those who say to remarry in church would cause offence to the Christian conscience may find that failure to do so causes greater offence.

The report thinks such remarriage of divorced persons is theologically, rationally, and pastorally desirable. It notes that other Anglican Churches, elsewhere in the Anglican Communion, have recently introduced such remarriage rites, for example the Anglican Church in Rhodesia, Zambia, Malawi and Botswana introduced such a remarriage rite in 1969. This is an area of Africa missioned by Anglican Catholics, originally in the Universities Mission to Central Africa until it amalgamated with the Society for the Propagation of the Gospel to form the United Society for the Propagation of the Gospel (USPG) in 1965. This mission organisation still provides some funds for clergy and bishops in this part of Africa, and is still Catholic in emphasis. Acceptance of remarriage in church here is not too surprising, for Anglican Catholics claim to be part of the Catholic Church which they see as consisting of the three church groups which preserve Apostolic Succession through the bishops, and a sacramental approach to their religion. The Eastern Orthodox Churches, which meet these criteria of 'catholicity', have always allowed such remarriages. The Central African Church used these liturgies in devising its own rite for remarriage. The Lambeth Conference, which meets every ten years, will have to discuss this matter again in 1978.

The Church of England will no doubt eventually introduce such a remarriage rite, thus enabling people who wish to re-marry, who otherwise have to go to a Registrar's Office, to have the ritual in a church. The Church Union, an organisation in England of Catholic-oriented laity and clergy (11,000 laity, 2,000 clergy members) condemned the proposals to allow re-marriage in a church in 1971. This was presumably to follow the stern Roman Catholic attitude to these matters within the Anglican Catholic movement in England. However, the possi-bility for change exists here, as in the Central African Church, by examining Eastern Orthodox practices in these matters.

Another area where the official Church of England attitude is firm, and in this case is in keeping with the State's approach, is in relation to 'marriages' between people of the same sex who wish to have their union publicly affirmed and brought before God, in the case of Christian believers who are homosexual. In America there are a number of Gay Churches; some of these are liberal protestant in orientation, but others are more 'Catholic' in the sense defined above. For example, the American Orthodox Church has solemnised marriages between two males in 1971.[32] The Archbishop of Canterbury, Michael Ramsay, said in 1972 that he did not see the Church of England giving its blessing to marriages between two people of the same sex. 'Because the Christian Church gives its blessing to the best and perfect use of sex, which is the union of a man and woman in marriage. We confine our blessings to that.'[33] Unlike some Churches in America, excluding the Anglicans as yet, and many other Churches too, the Church of England has little comfort for homosexual men or women, for theirs is an 'im-perfect form' of sexuality, not the best. They must live without permanent relationships, or within relationships which cannot be blessed by the Church. This is obviously only of concern to homosexual members of the Church of England and other Churches, as others would not carry any burden of guilt, deriving from their non-existent religion. It should perhaps be added that the Church of England bishops were pushing for the law about male homosexuality to be repealed in the late 1950s, thus enabling the Wolfenden Report to feel able to recommend the changes they did, and the law to be changed in 1966 to allow homosexual males over twenty-one to have sexual relations together in private.

The Church of England's teaching on human sexuality and its use has been changing throughout this century. It has shifted from condemning the use of birth control in 1908, to a position where it may well alter the marriage service itself to put less emphasis on marriage and sexuality being primarily for the procreation of children.[34] (A new Liturgical Commission group is to report on the Marriage Service in 1973.) As can be seen, however, from the statement quoted by the Archbishop of Canterbury, the Church sees sex as being properly based only in a married relationship between two people of the opposite sex. Opinion within the Church of England is divided on these matters of sexual morality, ranging from permissive liberals, through a moderately permissive attitude as exemplified by Bishop John Robinson, once Bishop of Woolwich, to the strictest line possible, as 'hard' as the sternest Roman Catholic sex moralist. Most clergy and laity do not hold clearly articulated positions on these matters, being fairly tolerant of divorce, and even remarriage, and of birth control, but seeing the monogamous family as the basis of society.[35]

An interesting omission in much of the work on marriage within the Christian Churches, and the Church of England in particular, is in the area of choice of partner. This has ceased to be a major problem in England, although not for some of the immigrant groups, such as Cypriots, who belong to the Greek Orthodox Church. There is of course the value to which most active members of the Church of England subscribe, that is that sexual intercourse before marriage is morally wrong. The choice of partner is to be made, it is assumed, on the basis of the mutual love of the two people, not by arranged marriage by the parents, as in the society of ancient Palestine. This mutual love must have some erotic component presumably, but the Church as an official body, and more importantly at the level of local youth clubs, is highly ambivalent about people having much sexual experience before they are married, or at least engaged. Most of the active Church of England people interviewed in the London area in the late sixties, in a non-representative sample, aged under twenty-eight years, thought sexual relations during engagement were 'O.K.' but they felt negatively about people making their choice of partner after some sexual experience with a number of other partners. In other words, choice of partner is initially thought to be based on other factors than sexual compatibility. Two people with limited, or no other, sexual experience, especially in the case of the females, choose one another and form some commitment and then become engaged to be married, and in this situation can start a tentative exploration of their sexuality.

The Church of England remains uneasy about sexuality. It is perceived by young people, who do not regard themselves as active members of it although they may well have been baptised into the C. of E., as having a condemnatory attitude towards sexual experience between teenagers. Such people find it difficult to see the Church of England, or any other Church, as a place they might seek advice about sexual matters before they are married—and fairly practical, physiological advice is what is often required, in matters concerning forms of birth control, where they can be purchased, masturbation for both sexes, homosexuality, pregnancy, and what to do about involvements between people.[36]

In the past there was a cultural assumption among the English that brides, and even bridegrooms, should be virgins before being married in church. Some people in closely knit communities, where it is known that a couple have been having sexual relations together, perhaps because the girl has become pregnant, still feel they should not be married in a church, but in a registrar's office. In such a community, there is something not quite as respectable about a registrar's office as the Church of England for a wedding.[37]

The Church's ambivalence about sexuality, seeing it as good and yet something which must not be overdone, something to be practised only in special relationships, prevents it being of much help as a local advice centre to many young people who are not married. There are some clergy whose attitudes about sexuality are in fact quite different from what many of these young people would expect, and they could be of help on a practical level, but their role as priests of the Church of England is not something which only they define. It is defined also by older laity in the local church, and by the young themselves, who operate with a stereotypical model of the 'clergyman' which is very difficult for any clergyman to overcome.[38]

In a society in which property is to be transmitted to legitimate heirs of the father, it is important to be able to know exactly who the father is. It is easier to trace a mother because the biological process of birth, and post-natal dependence, makes the role clearer. It is less easy with the father of the child, unless there are tight controls over the sexual activity of the male, restricting it to only one woman. In a society in which property has traditionally passed through the male line of a family, the need to know about the father of children is crucial. This basic structural fact about middle-class families in England over the last few centuries underpins the moral attitudes of the Church of England to these matters. Not in a simple, direct way, but because a national Church cannot teach for long values which run contrary to the property relations of the society, and the norms needed by the dominant propertied class in that society to perpetuate their inheritance customs. The Church of England's teachings have only been relaxed in a situation where it has been found, over the life of a generation or more, that, for instance, birth control methods are sufficiently reliable, and in use by middle-class families on quite a wide scale, and that it is therefore safe to change without creating an uproar among its major supporters, the English middle class. For this reason the Church will always lag behind what is current practice among the most advanced section of the middle class, in order not to offend and disrupt its relationship with the broad, and relatively older, sections of the middle classes.

The working class have very little property, if any, to transmit to their children, so therefore they are much less concerned with the problem of knowing absolutely accurately, and without any shadow of doubt, who is the father of a particular child. The Church of England's moral teachings reflect the concerns of the middle classes, and are more remote from the moral concerns of the working classes. In the working classes the problem is more about who is expected to support the mother and child; which male is to be expected to pay for the costs of this. Or failing this, how to develop a welfare system which will allow the whole community to pay for the upkeep of mothers and children, who have no working father-husbands. As the taxes for the upkeep of these fatherless, husband-less families comes from the middle classes in large part, the middle class will tend to use their moral value system to condemn the behaviour of the working-class women, and men, who get themselves into this position. The Church can find itself being used, by laity, clergy, bishops, and local dignitaries, to attack this behaviour from a middle-class perspective.[39]

DEATH AND BURIAL

Very few people are buried without a religious rite of some kind. Geoffrey Gorer in his study *Death, Grief and Mourning* found only 2 out of his sample of 359 had been buried without a religious rite. Over 70 per cent of those interviewed by Gorer in England used the Church of England rite for the burial.[40] Yet it seems from his material that few held orthodox beliefs about life after death. A quarter did not believe in any life after death (in a 1963 Gallup Poll 53 per cent positively believed in life after death).[41] The others were not very religiously oriented in their replies, and were not 'orthodox' in Gorer's sense, in that they did not mention judgement by God. Only 11 out of 359 held orthodox beliefs including the belief in an after-life and God's judgement.[42] Quite a number of replies mentioned some form of reincarnation as among their beliefs.

The Church of England allows cremation as well as burial, and in 1963 41 per cent were cremated in Britain. (Roman Catholics could not be cremated until a new ruling was issued by the Pope in 1963 allowing cremation. Orthodox Jews cannot be cremated.)

Gorer found that in spite of the high use made of the Church of England rite, very little mention was made of the clergy as playing an active part in the funeral arrangements, or in contact with the bereaved family.[43]

This is no doubt because the process is increasingly handled by funeral directors, who are hired by the bereaved to make the arrangements for the burial of the body. The funeral director now, especially in towns, is concerned with the laying out of the body, putting the body into a coffin, and arranging for cremation or burial. In the past, local communities in England had a local person, usually a woman, who was known to possess the skills necessary to do the laying out of the body. This was often done in the house where the person died, the body often remaining there until the day of the funeral, usually two or three days after the death. This length of time is longer than in many parts of the world where the climate, probably as much as cultural norms, necessitates the disposal of the body on the same day, or the very next day after the death. Dead bodies are in most, if not all human societies, 'impure' objects. There is something potentially polluting about them, and so people who handle the actual dead body usually have less prestige than those who perform rites around them, like priests, or who certify death, like doctors. The priests perform ritual at the burial, but are not expected to handle the dead body at all. Some social distance between the priest and the dead is to be anticipated, and this could extend to the bereaved family, in the immediate aftermath of the death itself.

Bryan Wilson makes the point that death is becoming a private matter in modern England, and is less a group, public, issue that it used to be. Hence the loss of public mourning rites after burial, in the form of abstention from certain activities, and the wearing of special clothing, especially by women, which Gorer reported and documented. 'From being a socially recognised inevitability, death has become an embarrassing private trauma in which almost any outside solace, except from intimates, has become an intrusion.'[44] Death remains an event with which the family has to cope. The family has perhaps itself become the private sphere, *par excellence*, and ritual events of the life-cycle type belong to this social group above all others. This overlooks the fact that family life is not entirely privatised, that the State and the Church still regulate its affairs. It is a basic social institution in industrial consumer society and as such cannot be ignored.

Funerals, and the associated gathering after the burial rite itself, do have functions for the family as an institution. The loss of a member needs to be marked by all who are regarded as members of the family, and who regard themselves as members of the family. This is why, in spite of the fact that so many people will say they dislike attending funerals, they usually nevertheless do attend, for not to do so would be perceived by significant others in the family group as implying the person no longer regarded themselves as a member of the family and kin group, particularly if absence became a regular occurrence.

One aspect of funerals which neither Gorer nor anyone else has explored is the meaning which they have for people. This meaning will be at a level which may not emerge in a single interview of the kind Gorer conducted. There is an increasing mass of statistics on what people have said they believe, but very little which attempts to explore meaning-structures, how these beliefs and practices fit together to produce a world view, not of a highly intellectualised kind, but one which may be operating nevertheless.[45] One idea worth further exploration is related to the ideas of spirits and ghosts, and even luck—people probably want to bury their dead 'properly' to avoid them being restless after death. This would come near a very different idea from what Gorer, for example, calls orthodox, namely that whether there be a life after death or not, the spirit of a dead person can be restless, unless properly laid out to rest with the body. People are fascinated by the idea of séances, and spiritualist contacts with the dead, in modern industrial England. Many feel the dead are best left alone, but some do try to contact them at one time or another. The burial ritual would then be important for such a group holding a view of the world which included the existence of spirits.[46] And people wish to be buried in *consecrated* ground.

At this point it is useful to look at a report produced by a Commission convened by the Bishop of Exeter, on exorcism in the Church of England.[47] There had been something of an outburst in the Press, in 1963, when it was reported that there were exorcists who practised exorcism within that Church. It was seen as white magic which belonged to the Middle Ages, perhaps, but not to the twentieth century. The report recommended that there should be training courses for clergy on exorcism, and there should be a trained exorcist among the clergy in every diocese in England. The rite involves the casting out of demons from people or places. The first thing about this is that it is accepted as a part of the Christian world view, by these Anglicans at least, that there exist demons as well as the Devil. In the 1963 Gallup Poll 36 per cent of the respondents believed in the Devil, 46 per cent did not believe in the Devil, and 18 per cent did not know what to think.[48] There is, therefore, a substantial section of the English population who believe in these beings. It is worth noticing that the report also makes claims for the rationality of the Christian religion. 'Evil, a distortion of right orderliness, proceeds from created, intelligent wills, either human or demonic. Both are possible sources of evil . . .'

The New Testament . . . assumes the existence of evil powers which have their origin in personalities but which prefer to manifest themselves in disturbances such as disease, bad social conditions, political corruption, and mistaken cultural assumptions . . . Moreover, since the Logos is the Ratio of God, true reason is of divine origin. That which turns away from God becomes increasingly non-rational and so sub-rational . . . Demonic forces lead to a confusion and degradation of personalities.[49]

The writers of the report at least do not see their ideas of demonic evil as non-rational, rather non-rationality is a product of such evil. The difficulty with the idea of evil demons is that it is strictly unnecessary, and does not follow from the definition of evil given in the report, nor from the description of types of evil. The definition and the examples of evil are unobjectionable and reasonable. But they need not imply the existence of demons who cause the evil to anyone who does not want to accept that they exist. The claim for their existence rests, for Christians, in revelation, and in the above quotation the New Testament is not mentioned for just historical reasons. It is really being appealed to as an authority of the Christian revelation. Whether it is reasonable to accept such sources of revelation is a matter that cannot be argued out here, suffice to say that the authors of the report would claim it is reasonable, and thus they enter the arena of rational discussion. They would claim there is no reason to trust our reasoning processes without some 'over-beliefs' not contained within reasoning itself. Their over-belief is that reason can be used because it is of God, whose existence can be at least *pointed to* from other directions in any case.

There is no point, therefore, in seeing the idea of 'demons' as primitive and non-rational, as many sociologists among others are tempted to do.[50] Further analysis shows that the beliefs and rituals are not quite so non-rational, or superstitious, as may be supposed, as far as the religious virtuosi at least are concerned.

Some social scientists, following psycho-analytic insights, might prefer to see the ideas as ways of dealing with unconscious forces in human existence, which can appear to *take possession* of someone when they affect actual behaviour. Again we have no simple way of knowing that such unconscious forces are really there; it is a way of seeking some understanding of behaviour and phenomena which otherwise are inexplicable within our twentieth-century materialist, technological, world view. Some psychiatrists are willing to admit the possibility that exorcism and other religious ritual may 'work' for some people. There was a consultant psychiatrist on the Commission which produced the Anglican Report on Exorcism. The report is careful to distinguish spiritual problems, where exorcism may be appropriate, from physical and psychological illness. And they say that

The apparent failure of medical treatment should not necessarily be taken as evidence that the illness is spiritual. Psychological medicine is still limited in scope, empirical in form, and rapidly changing. Paradoxically the relative success of medical treatment should not be considered as excluding a residual spiritual problem, requiring spiritual treatment. The diagnosis of demonic 'possession' must rest on precise and positive criteria.[51]

These criteria are not spelled out in the report. The section would seem to imply that there is a distinction between psychological illness and spiritual problems, such as 'possession'. Therefore, it is not possible to say that for these Christians all 'demons' are unconscious forces, for presumably these latter are potentially amenable to psychological medicine's empirical, therapeutic methods. Carl Jung seems to have himself suggested that there could be a category of problems for which the priest was more suitable than the psychiatrist.[52]

The Church of England, like the Roman Catholic and Eastern Orthodox Churches, has a ritual for the *anointing* of the sick. This would imply that spiritual actions of this kind can be added to other forms of medicine. They are not mutually exclusive. The priest should not be called in when the doctor has failed to cure the patient, but for the spiritual comfort the priest can offer in his own right. Many Anglican laity attend faith-healing services held by people that the clergy often think are theologically suspect, in that they do promise help where doctors fail, as though God or Jesus were some kind of magical alternative to medicine. Nevertheless, because laity do attend these services, the Church élites are concerned to revive the rituals contained in the Anglican Prayer Book for visiting the sick. The exorcism report contained a form for the laying on of hands for sick people, and a form for anointing the sick with holy oil, specially consecrated for the purpose.

All of these ritual actions concerned with life-cycle events and crises in living involve assumptions that the ritual action can be of help. To the religious élites this is understood to be primarily a spiritual matter, but many ordinary lay users do not seem to make such clear-cut distinctions between real material benefits, such as health being restored, or a poltergeist ceasing 'its' activity, and spiritual matters. Burial in consecrated ground, or scattering of ashes in consecrated places with the correct ritual being used, are particularly important, as well as the rituals of visiting the sick, and exorcism. Baptism may also be used on the basis of similar assumptions—that babies need dedicating to God, to give them a good start, and to remove any evil propensities present at birth. 'It is best to be on the safe side.' Marriage may also involve the idea that a couple should start their married life together with a blessing from God. The churching of women after childbirth is also a ritual performed 'just in case'. By giving thanks to God for safe deliverance, the mother can feel that nothing has been missed out which might affect her health or the new-born baby's, because she did not give thanks to God.

One of the major differences within Anglicanism, and within the Church of England, which has grown up in the last hundred years, after being a highly divisive issue during the Reformation period, concerns *prayers for the dead*. The Roman Catholic notion of purgatory seemed to justify the idea that it was import-ant and meaningful to pray for the soul of the departed. There were many corrupt practices around this doctrine, such as the sale of indulgences which enabled the purchaser to buy himself out of so many days, or years, in purgatory—a state of existence after death, where people were punished for their wrong doings before going to heaven. The Church of England had always condemned this doctrine of purgatory in its teaching, and in the official Thirty-nine Articles (Article XXII).

Nevertheless, people have wanted to perform ritual actions, including some kind of prayers for the dead, without assuming the belief in purgatory. This has been marked by the use of memorial services for relatives, and for national, or local figures. The Anglo-Catholic movement led to the introduction of Requiem Masses again in the Church of England, and other Anglican Churches in the world. The Church of England had retained the Feast of All Saints, which was a special occasion for giving thanks for the lives of the saints, and remembering them, although they were, of course, dead. The Anglo-Catholic clergy re-introduced All Souls Day, 2 November, when the dead of the parish are remembered and named, and God is asked to give them rest and peace. 'Rest eternal grant unto them, O Lord; and let light perpetual shine upon them.' Evangelicals in the Church of England have traditionally been against these prayers for the dead, and especially against naming dead people who are being prayed for; it all seems to them too much like the Romish doctrine of purgatory.

A recent Church of England Liturgical Commission report on the burial of the dead[53] is primarily concerned with this problem, and seeks to find a form of burial service which all will use in the Church of England. It concludes that prayer for the dead is not ruled out by Article XXII, but that such prayers should remain optional in the new rite. The report also says that communion at funerals should be encouraged, and not discouraged, as had been the case in the past very often outside Anglo-Catholic parishes.[54]

Rituals and prayers for dead people have not disappeared under modern industrial conditions, and indeed they are on the increase within the Church of England. There are many reasons for this. The Church of England has become more ritually developed in the twentieth century anyway, but specifically with relation to rituals to do with the dead there seems to be an acceptance by more clergy that people want something to do in this area, and that if the Church does not provide something, the laity will go to other, less orthodox, spiritualist meetings and séances. The rituals seem to be needed to cope with the emotions of the bereaved, rather than to express intellectually held beliefs about the state of humans after their death. Some members of the Church of England do not believe, so they say, in a life after death, and yet some of these will nevertheless attend rituals to do with the dead. It is as though they feel that if nothing is done, the dead may not attain rest and peace, but possibly haunt the world as ghosts, or in some other way. So they will deny a belief in an after-life, because their idea is not of life after death; their belief system does include the idea that the dead may not achieve final rest and peace. The rituals they perform may help the dead person attain such rest. If the burial ritual is not carried out, or some prayers said that God may give them rest, then there could be bad consequences for the dead person, in that they do not find eternal rest. This belief system is not Christian to many theologians, and it is one which appears in other parts of the world. It is, however, one

18 *Above*: Peter Brook's production of *A Midsummer Night's Dream*, 1972, Royal Shakespeare Company. Jennie Stoller (Helena) and Zhivilia Roche (Hermia) using their bodies more aggressively than has been usual in previous productions of the play. *Left*: Use of trapezes for Oberon (Alan Howard) and Puck (Robert Lloyd).

Photographs by Morris Newcombe

Press Associa

19 Demonstration at the opening night of *Jesus Christ, Superstar* outside the Palace Theatre, London, 1972.

which some people do feel, and find meaningful. Unfortunately little is known empirically about these beliefs concerning ghosts, rest after death, and what survivors should do after the death of someone. The above is based on observation in a number of Church of England parishes, in the country and in London, and on informal interviews. It is not possible on this basis to know how widespread these views are. Again it should be pointed out that rituals are often performed for less than clearly articulated reasons, whatever they may be. If a ritual concerned with the dead provides for handling feelings that survivors have, such as guilt about not doing enough for the deceased when they were alive, or grief, or anxiety about death in general, or the possibility of some kind of return in ghostly form of the dead person, then such rituals will continue to be performed.[55]

CONCLUSION

These rituals are examples of what Max Weber termed a 'salvation religion' offering release from suffering and using what he termed 'magical sacramental grace'.[56] These types of religion appeal to the non-privileged classes, although the modern proletariat turns to political and economic change as a means of salvation from their condition. 'Other things being equal, classes with high social and economic privilege will scarcely be prone to evolve the idea of salvation. Rather, they assign to religion the primary function of legitimising their own life pattern and situation in the world.'[57] The Church of England can be seen to have certainly done the latter for highly privileged classes in the past, and because of this has lost the more sacramental and soteriological rituals, compared with, say, the Roman Catholic Church, in societies with peasantries. The Anglo-Catholic Ritualists have been the group which has done most to revive these aspects of Christianity within the Church of England, and Anglicanism more generally. This group has been the main one to contact some sections of the working class, who for one reason or another do not find socialism enough for them presumably because it offers no immediate salvation in terms of release and help during suffering in the individual's own life

K

cycle. Thus it is at crisis and transition points in the life cycle that much ritual action continues, even among the working class in England. Many lower middle-class people too, in both rural and urban areas, are likely to feel a need for such ritual action from time to time, especially during illness or death in the family. Many of the differences within the Church of England about ritual action and the nature of Christianity can be seen as being produced by differences among the members in terms of social and economic privileges.

Chapter Seven

Aesthetic Ritual

An analysis of the relations between ritual in the performing arts and in religion is more relevant in the context of this book than a fuller analysis of the arts from a sociological point of view. Specific cases of works which relate to the general process of the separation out of aesthetic ritual from religious ritual in European Christian societies will be examined.

The main thesis is that where a religion develops an orientation towards a supernatural realm, and a consequent distrust of this world, its ritual system will become unspontaneous and unsensual. This leads to the growth of an alternative ritual system which does encourage and allow some degree of spontaneity and sensuality among those social groups whose material and 'ideal' interests are not served by the more ascetic religion. The growth of dance halls, pop music, and variety shows among the working classes in the last hundred years is one example.

Sections of the middle class, especially intellectuals, have become detached from orthodox church teachings, sometimes because the teachings have been proved mistaken by science, sometimes because of the conservative nature of the values of the Churches, and the lack of intellectual openness in their belief systems. Such groups have been the patrons of the aesthetic ritual-symbol systems which have grown up outside the main Churches, and these rituals have been a satisfactory substitute for religious ritual. Indeed because of their acceptance of sensuality and the body, they have been better for precisely this reason in the eyes of many of these people.[1]

The majority of the working class have been historically outside the influence of the orthodox Churches and have developed their own cultures and rituals with more spontaneity and acceptance of the body. There are, nevertheless, considerable Christian overtones in many working-class rituals, as will be seen later.

A new process is developing which is different from the above. This is the use of religious symbols and rituals in aesthetic rituals. The process may not be one which in any way strengthens the numerical size of the orthodox Churches, but one which makes use of religious symbols and rituals for aesthetic purposes. There is, however, an element of the recovery of the sacred, of numinous experience, in some of these works, and any rigid borderline between a purely aesthetic experience and a religious one becomes difficult to draw. The search for meaning can and does go on in the sphere of aesthetic rituals, and this produces ritual events which are religious in that they approach an attitude of worship, as in Britten's *War Requiem*, for example. The main distinction remains nevertheless; the rituals of the Churches are anti-sensual; many aesthetic rituals, primarily dancing, allow for more sensuality, in the sense of a positive approach to the body.[2]

The method to be used is to relate sociological generalities to specific works with a high ritual element, in order to illuminate these works and to give some empirical bite to the sociological analysis. Each of the works chosen for analysis has special characteristics in relation to the central problems under examination. Many other works could have been chosen, but there is so much to be said about the relation of the arts to ritual, myth, religion, and values, that some selection is an absolute necessity.

The approach taken here is not reductionist. It is methodologically akin to the sociology of literature as developed by Lucien Goldmann. Raymond Williams has argued in an article on 'Literature and Sociology' that the crude Marxist approach failed because it could not handle the actual works produced by individual authors. Particular key works should be considered in detail; Raymond Williams says that Goldmann held that some works realise a world view at its most coherent and most adequate.

We should not then mainly study peripheral relations; correspondence of content and background; overt social relations between writers and readers. We should study, in the greatest literature, the organising categories, the essential structures, which give such works their unity, their specific aesthetic character, their strictly literary quality; and which at the same time reveal to us the maximum possible consciousness of the social group—in real terms the social class—which finally created them, in and through their individual authors.[3]

In relation to aesthetic ritual especially, these same principles can apply. In Goldmann's terms, aesthetic works deal more with *potential consciousness* than with actual consciousness. Religious ritual similarly may sometimes be about potentiality, as some modern Catholics would argue is the case with Christian rituals.[4]

Aesthetic rituals are usually created by a group, with perhaps one person central to the conception of the whole. Rituals are more difficult to analyse than literature because there is no common public form which can be referred to by authors and readers. This is a real technical difficulty; photographs and recordings help, together with any text and written descriptions.

RITUAL IN THE ARTS

It would be possible to say that all activity which involves viewing and appreciating the arts is aesthetic ritual action, in that a group of people, or separate individuals, relate to symbols of an aesthetic type. At bare minimum this is ritual action, as distinct from action of a rational, technical kind. Having said this, however, it is possible, and necessary, to go on to differentiate within the arts, on the basis of the fact that some works of art are more 'ritualistic' than others. Those works which draw on myths, either from ancient Greece, Teutonic or Celtic Europe, Christianity, Hinduism, or whatever, and involve some kind of performance from artists, are the most crucial examples of ritual arts, or what are called here *aesthetic rituals*.

Paintings may well involve mythic symbols, and are to that

degree an important part of the process by which mythic, numinal consciousness is articulated and expressed in modern society. However, they are of less importance for social groups; they are usually now produced by one person, and looked at by the individual, or even purchased by a person for himself and his family. The so-called performing arts involve groups of artists to perform them, and they involve a social group, an audience, to be responsive to them, and to co-operate with the actual performers in enacting the work. The group processes involved are of some interest in themselves, and in their effects on the works of art performed and written.

An audience builds up an emotional rapport among its members, and between itself and the performers of the aesthetic ritual. There is a sense of irritation with members of an audience who will not make the necessary emotional connection with the others and with the performers, in a theatre or a concert, especially when this results in outwardly expressed action, such as talking in the 'wrong' places, sleeping or scowling. This is true of young people watching a pop group, where the expectation is that members of an audience will express great enthusiasm, as well as of middle-class theatre and concert audiences. A group in an art gallery never quite builds up this degree of emotional structure, because the act of looking at paintings is not bounded by space and time in the same way that an aesthetic performance is. Ikons, however, are clearly ritual objects for orthodox Christians, who perform ritual actions in front of them, such as lighting a candle and praying. For modern Westerners, and Communists in the USSR, for instance, they are not religious ritual objects, but aesthetic objects, which may nevertheless have the capacity to communicate something of a 'numinous' atmosphere to people who are not believers.

TENSIONS BETWEEN THE ARTS AND RELIGION

The tensions between the arts and religion are to be discussed in the context of European civilisation and Christianity. 'The free Greek, who set himself upon the pinnacle of Nature, could procreate art from very joy in manhood; the Christian, who impartially cast aside both Nature and himself could only sacrifice to his God on the altar of renunciation . . .' (Richard Wagner[5]).

Wagner's reaction against Christianity was founded on its rejection of the body and nature, and its overemphasis on the spirit and mind, in short the Manichean influence within Western Christianity. In so far as Christianity has contained other elements which can be more body-accepting, often expressed today in liberal Protestantism and liberal Catholicism, then it can lead to an art less preoccupied with escape from this world into another realm of supernatural spirit, unencumbered by matter.

Some Christians have often played no small part in reform and radical movements of opinion about sexual matters, especially in Britain and the USA. However, such influences have tended not to be linked in any clear and explicit way with the arts.

The problematic relationship of ritual action and attitudes to sexuality lies behind the growth of the arts outside the Churches in Europe. Groups concerned with aesthetic ritual who did not share the Christian attitude to sexuality, found that they increasingly had to develop their arts outside the Church's control. Theatres became in a very real sense 'temples' for a religion other than that of the Christianity of the Churches.

In an interesting analysis Geradus van der Leeuw sees theatre and Christian Churches as in a state of strain in their relationship to one another, because they represent two different religions in Europe:

We do not see theatre and religion, but two different religions, one against another; the ancient fertility religion of the *sacer ludus*, with its candor and sexual symbols, and the new ascetic religion of Christendom. The theatre must pay for its fidelity to the ancient primitive religious forms with the hostility of the new religions.[6]

Music-halls in England can be seen in relation to the anti-body attitudes of the Christian Churches, especially in the late nineteenth, and early years of the twentieth, century when the music-hall was strong as a form of entertainment. Music-hall involved a high degree of audience participation in the form of singing and shouting out in response to remarks and jokes from the artists on the stage. Often the audience was drinking and sometimes eating too, and was in this respect far removed from the ascetic values of evangelical Christianity. Something of the way music-hall values were in contra-distinction to those of asceticism can be seen in the following quotation about Marie Lloyd (1885-1922).

> She preached the world and the flesh, and gloried in their being the very devil. Frank in gesture as Fielding was in phrase, her page of life was as outspoken and as sure. She relished and expounded those things which she knew to be dear to the common heart. She was adored by the lowest classes, by the middle people and by the swells. Marie broadened life and showed it, not as a mean affair of refusal and restraint, but as a boon to be lustily enjoyed. She redeemed us from virtue too straitlaced and her great heart cracked too soon. (James Agate, *Saturday Review*, 1922)

This is on the wall in the Aba Daba Music Hall at the Pindar of Wakefield pub in London, a music-hall revival begun in the late 1960s and early 1970s.

This type of revival of music-hall, as a form of live entertainment, in cities throughout England, is itself significant. It came after most people had become used to television and somewhat bored with it. The boredom seems to stem from the fact that people have to stay in with the rest of the family, rather than 'going out', dressing up for the occasion, and experiencing a break in normal routine as a result. Television allows for no audience participation; even the laughter is provided. Many people comment in conversations at music-halls that the experience is much richer and more rewarding than staying in to watch 'the telly'.

The later developments of music-hall took place in variety theatre, and then in variety shows, built around singers or comedians, finally transferred to television. A living audience adds a dimension which is lacking on television; watching a

20 London Contemporary Dance Theatre—*Eclipse*. Dancers—
Robert North and Irene Dilks.

21   Dutch National Ballet with Rudolf Nureyev in *Apollo*, London,
1969.

Press Association

22   Gymnastics. Royal Albert Hall, London, 1966. Aesthetic ritual—
       compare with ballet (see picture opposite).

23 London Contemporary
Dance Theatre—*Kontakion*
Dancer—William Louther.

Photographs by Anthony Crickm

variety show on television is not a social event in the way a visit to a live show is.[7]

A Midsummer Night's Dream, directed by Peter Brook (1971-72, Royal Shakespeare Company)
The key elements in this play, from the point of view of ritual, centre on the way Peter Brook used the actors' bodies, rather than just concentrating on the literary qualities of the lines. He also used circus and showman techniques, such as the trapezes for Puck and Oberon, the stilts which Puck uses, and the spinning plate to act as the magic potions. The two young women used their bodies in ways which were more virile, aggressive and sexual than is usually the case. No longer were they female eunuchs!

The music was created by the actors themselves. There was a guitar player who strolled on to the stage when the actors were going to sing. The singing was sensual; the voices were not highly trained singing voices, by any means. Drums were put at the top of the front of the stage and used effectively—rhythmic, noisy and brash. Act One ended with glitter, a sense of festivity, and was the one time that Mendelssohn's music for the play was used, with tremendous effect.

At the end the actors, following a line at the end of the play itself—'Give me your hands, if we be friends'—came down among the audience to shake their hands and ask how the play had been, and then returned to the stage for the applause. The actors also applauded the audience. Here the normal barriers of conventional theatre were being transcended.

This production was one which, although in a sense fashionable and could easily date, will remain of lasting importance for the theatre and staging. Bodies were back in the theatre. It was a fusion of rough theatre and holy theatre; a revival of ideas developed by Meyerhold in Russia in the 1920s.[8] In that it represented life in the body, it has the central positive function of ritual for modern men and women, of showing ways of relating to the body. This is unlike literary theatre which treats people, via the actors, as people who only talk and feel through words, rather than through their bodies as a whole. It also attempted to overcome the social distance between actors and audience, more than is usual. This is much more developed in other *avant-garde* theatre groups, such as 'Liquid Theatre', but nevertheless it *was* a crucial development in making theatre a place for living ritual events.

THE RETURN TO RELIGION IN THE ARTS

Since the latter part of the nineteenth century, there has been some movement in the arts back to religion. There are numerous examples of this process. The ones here are chosen in terms of their centrality to the process being examined, i.e. aesthetic ritual and the return to religion. This may mean two things, which should be kept analytically distinct. On the one hand there is the artist himself who may come to talk of artistic creative action, which is at the centre of his life, in terms which sound, and are meant to sound, religious. For example, Igor Stravinsky: 'Thus the consummated work spreads to be communicated and finally flows back to its source. The cycle, then is closed. And that is how music comes to reveal itself as a form of communion with our fellow man—and with the Supreme Being.'[9]

This is distinct from the work of art itself, and its relation to religious consciousness. A work of art may be produced by a 'religious' artist and yet not be a work which is 'religious' in the sense that a Russian ikon is a religious work, or the works of artists and craftsmen in pre-literate societies, such as African masks and drums, are religious works of art. Sometimes the work is meant to be, and is used as, a religious ritual symbolic object, such as a piece of music for liturgical performance, e.g. Britten's *Missa Brevis* which is actually used in worship. Other works are more complex. For instance, Britten's *War Requiem* is not a liturgical work in the same way that *Missa Brevis* is, and yet it is in a sense close to a liturgical act of worship when performed.

The crucial point seems to be whether a work is *used* in acts of worship or not. An act of worship is built on the assumption that people present are there to worship God. However that is understood, it does imply some being 'God' to whom the worship is addressed. A work of art such as the *War Requiem* does not make this assumption. It can be appreciated by anyone prepared to make the effort to listen to it. It does not need the audience to interpret it as worship; indeed to so interpret it is to miss the aesthetic point of the tensions in the structure and the words, tensions which cannot be appreciated within a liturgical framework. Crucially, there is no liturgical action going on to accompany the music as there is at a 'real' Requiem Mass; the aesthetic form is so complex that it is to be listened to in its own right, not as part of a broader act of liturgical worship. Much music of the last two and half centuries, which looks religious because it uses religious words and forms, is not really *liturgical* music at all.

War Requiem, Benjamin Britten 1963[10]
In the *War Requiem* the English words of the poems of Wilfred Owen are interwoven with the Latin of the Requiem Mass; musically the two are in tension, as well as the feelings underlying the two sets of words. For example, at the end of the 'Dies Irae' section, the poem is searching for the meaning and asking if there can be any consolation for the death of a soldier friend:

Tenor Solo
  Move him,
  Move him into the sun—
  Gently its touch awoke him once,
  At home, whisp'ring of fields unsown
  Always it woke him, woke him even in France,
  Until this morning and this snow,
  If anything might rouse him now
  The kind old sun will know

Soprano and Chorus	English Translation
Lacrimosa dies illa	Ah! that day of tears and mourning!
Qua resurget ex favilla	From the dust of earth returning,

| Judicamus homo reus: | Man for judgement must prepare him: |
| Huic ergo parce Deus | Spare, O God, in mercy spare him! |

Tenor Solo
Think how it wakes the seeds—
Woke, once the clays of a cold star.
Are limbs, so dear-achieved, are sides,
Full-nerved—still warm—too hard to stir?
Was it for this the clay grew tall?

| Soprano Solo and Chorus | English Translation |
| Qua resurget ex favilla . . . | From the dust of earth returning |

Tenor Solo
Was it for this the clay grew tall?

| Soprano Solo and Chorus | English Translation |
| . . . Judicamus homo reus | . . . man for judgement must prepare him. |

Tenor Solo
—O what made fatuous sunbeams toil
To break earth's sleep at all?

Chorus	English Translation
Pie Jesu Domine, dona eis requiem	Lord, all-pitying, Jesu blest, grant them rest.
Amen.	Amen.

At the end of the work the music and words of the Mass and the poetry are united in some uneasy way:

The Baritone is singing the poem which ends the *War Requiem*:

I am the enemy you killed, my friend,
I knew you in this dark; for so you frowned
Yesterday through me as you jabbed and killed.
I parried; but my hands were loath and cold,
Let us sleep now . . .

Tenor and Baritone Solos
  Let us sleep now . . .

| Boys, Soprano Solos and Chorus | English Translation |
| In paradisum deductant te Angeli: | Into Paradise may the Angels lead thee: |

Chorus
  Requiescant in pace.   May they rest in Peace.
  Amen.   Amen.

Even without the music, it is possible to see here that the work depends on a juxtaposition of a secular man searching for meaning, wondering why, and the restfulness of the Latin, coming from an era of European history when 'God and His Angels' made sense, and so could console, and bring some meaning into human tragedy. The *War Requiem* is very near to an act of worship, but it doesn't quite ever become such; it is rather an act of quest for any meaning there might be in the wars of the twentieth century, an aesthetic act which attempts to articulate a response to the killing of people in modern war. People still look to the Church for consolation, but can it provide it in the twentieth century? There is no answer. Yet both the poem and the Latin Mass end with sleep and rest for those who have suffered. The connection seems to be at the level of emotion, even unconscious feelings. Both end with a state which is like Freud's Nirvana, a state of 'inactivity, rest or sleep, the twin brother of death'.[11]

Part of its initial success in England may well have been connected with the fact that it was a form of religious searching, in a neo-ritualised way, whatever its merits or otherwise as music. Attendance at a Bach, Haydn, Mozart, Beethoven or Verdi Mass may be seen similarly, although the element of quest and searching is missing. Yet it is this which is important for non-believers in the twentieth century. The *War Requiem* does not involve gesture or bodily movements on the part of the audience, and is therefore only neo-ritualistic in character.

Parsifal, Richard Wagner (1882)[12]

This opera is a crucial case in analysis of ritual action, for it stands in an almost unique position among modern operas, at least in Wagner's conception of it. It is *sacred Festival drama* (Bühnenweihtestspiel) as distinct from music-drama, which is in any case a distinct category from opera. It is the enactment of a myth, the myth of the Holy Grail, and involves ritual as a central part of the music-drama (ritual within what is already an aesthetic ritual). Scene Two of Act One consists of the ritual of Holy Communion which Parsifal watches, but cannot participate in, and does not understand. This ritual is enacted again in Scene Two of Act Three, this time with a transformed Parsifal as the central figure, the celebrant. There are many layers of meaning within *Parsifal*, but the one of interest here concerns the place of such ritual acts when performed in the opera house. A number of conventions seem to mark it out as sacred for the audience. One is its relation to the Christian religion, the religion of the greater part of the audience anyway. Wagner's other works are based more on non-Christian myths— *Tristan and Isolde*, *The Ring*, *The Flying Dutchman*, *Lohengrin*, *Tannhäuser*.

From the beginning, then, there is a deeper sense of 'respect' on the part of the audience for the mythic basis of the work. There are also different conventions governing applause for *Parsifal*—it is very muted at the end of Act One, indeed there should be none at all until the end of the music-drama, according to Wagner himself. (His wishes on this are subtly included in the Programme, in three languages, at Covent Garden.)

Nevertheless, it is not sacred ritual proper, for it does not involve the use of priests, that is, 'real' sacred figures who can 'really' consecrate the bread and wine in the Mass. This is further marked in the music itself. The music is really the crucial feature, although as in all Wagner's music-dramas the music and action on stage are very deeply related and interwoven with one another. This primary focus on the music (plus actions on stage) makes it a different setting from that of a ritual specifically for worship. Some of the experiences may overlap, in that both rituals may evoke the numinous, the Holy, but the point of

Parsifal is not to lead to worship, but aesthetic enjoyment and appreciation, and even perhaps, as a consequence, to a kind of therapeutic catharsis. (In neither this case, nor that of religious ritual, are unintended therapeutic consequences the real reason for the ritual, and it is very doubtful if rituals can effect their therapeutic action if attended and primarily performed for that reason.)

Wagner's *Parsifal* deals with the myth of the Holy Grail, and involves the portrayal of the Holy Communion ritual of Christianity on the stage. Wagner was attempting here to unify theatre, understood very much as a ritual-type of event with music. *Parsifal*, in particular, cross-cuts religious and aesthetic ritual categories, and yet helps in clarifying the nature of religious ritual worship, for *Parsifal* is not, in the last analysis, an act of worship in the full sense.

Myth is produced by groups of people living in relatively stable communities, by processes no one seems to have been able to conceptualise, let alone document. In the realm of the arts, the use of an established myth by recent artists makes analysis and documentation much more possible, but is obviously not to be seen as necessarily yielding any insights about myth creation as such. The use of myth by an artist is not the same as the emergence of a myth into the lives of people.

In the case of aesthetic rituals based on myth, the relation between myth and the ritual performance is clear, and it is the reverse of what is often said by anthropologists and others about myth and ritual. Anthony Wallace, for instance, says ritual is primary, myth follows.[13] Yet in the aesthetic rituals of concern here, the reverse is the case. The myth is known about first, and a work created to articulate it further, in a more ritual form.

An interesting case of the use of a mythic theme in pop entertainment developed in the early 1970s, with the rock-music 'operas' *Godspell* and *Jesus Christ, Superstar*.

Jesus Christ, Superstar, A. Lloyd Webber and Tim Rice (1970)[14]
Jesus Christ, Superstar deals with the nature of charisma. How did Jesus manage to make such an impact before the days

of mass media? As the voice of Judas asks at the end of the opera:

> Everytime I look at you I don't understand
> Why you let the things you did get so out of hand
> You'd have managed better if you'd had it planned
> Why'd you choose such a backward time and such a strange land?
> If you'd come today you would have reached a whole nation
> Israel in 4 B.C. had no mass communication
> Don't you get me wrong—I only want to know

Choir

> Jesus Christ, Jesus Christ
> Who are you? What have you sacrificed?
> Jesus Christ Superstar
> Do you think you're what they say you are?

At another point in the opera, Jesus is in the Garden of Gethsemane, the crowd is seemingly made up of journalists:

Crowd

> Tell me Christ how you feel tonight
> Do you plan to put up a fight?
> Do you feel that you've had the breaks?
> What would you say were your big mistakes?
> Do you think that you may retire?
> Did you think you would get much higher?
> How do you view your coming trial?
> Have your men proved at all worthwhile?

Again the theme recurs in the wine song of the Apostles, at the Last Supper:

> . . .
> Always hoped that I'd be an apostle
> Knew that I could make it if I tried
> Then when we retire we can write the gospels
> So they'll still talk about us when we've died.

This rock opera is not a liturgical work, any more than the *War Requiem*. It is primarily an aesthetic ritual which uses Jesus and his death as its story. However, the death of Jesus remains

24 Brass band. This one is a Salvation Army band, similar to those found in many working-class communities.

25 These pictures show the use of union banners (above) and a mask (of the landlord) (below) in working-class protest marches and demonstrations.

part of the great myth in societies influenced by Christianity. Just as anthropologists would study the way the myths of a culture change, and the new types of adaptation that emerge under changing social, political and economic conditions, so with the Jesus myth in our culture, sociologists and/or anthropologists must examine the ways in which it is used in rituals, such as this rock opera.

It would seem that the writers of the rock opera were struck by the charismatic qualities of Jesus, and the difficulties of communicating in an age devoid of mass media. How did his influence spread without the type of glamour attaching to 'Stars' in modern industrial capitalism? He must have been something different to have had the influence he has had.

Was he, as Pilate suggests, a self-destructive, misguided martyr?

> Don't let me stop your great self-destruction
> Die if you want to you misguided martyr . . .

Jesus' own song in the Garden of Gethsemane suggests a sacrificial victim (he is talking to God):

> . . .
> Alright I'll die!
> Just watch me die!
> See how I die!
> . . .
> I will drink your cup of poison, nail me to your cross and
>   break me
> Bleed me, beat me, kill me, take me now—before I change
>   my mind.

The opera has been a great success in America, both as a long-playing record (it was top of the American LP charts for months during 1971) and as a show on Broadway. In 1971 it was much more successful in these terms than in Britain, where the work was written.

Many groups in Britain seemed to be unsure how to respond to it. Christians tended to want to listen to it as a piece of sacred music—which did not sound quite right to British ears. Others

L

treated it as a dance record. According to some Anglican priests who had played it in church youth clubs, many people did not feel able to dance to it, yet some of their agnostic friends did dance to it in their homes.[15]

A work such as this reflects the ambiguous state of the Christian myth in industrial society; it retains a fascination for people for no matter how good or indifferent people find the music of the opera, it has an extra fascination for many people, especially older people perhaps, because it is about Jesus Christ. Another rock opera, *Catch my Soul*, which is a rock version of *Othello*, has somewhat less publicity and appeal than *Jesus Christ, Superstar* because it is not related to such a central myth of the culture of Britain or America. Myth relates a sacred history.[16]

Jesus Christ, Superstar has achieved a remarkable feat—it expresses a mythic theme of Christianity, sacrifice, in terms of a unique aesthetic form of industrial society, rock dance music. Theatre has kept alive the primitive religion of Europe, with its sexual symbolism and relation to the body; a rock opera is the modern form of this. Never before has theatre used its own forms to express such important mythic themes. Until *Jesus Christ, Superstar*, people seem to have seen it as irreverent to do this. It is interesting that this may be why the rock opera was so successful in the United States first, in a culture where the notion of 'sacred music' is not so deep-rooted as in Britain. This work expresses the myth in terms of the body, the erotic, by using 'rock' music.

Jesus Christ, Superstar and *Godspell* are both rock musicals using the life of Jesus as a basis for the lyrics. They are important in marking the meeting of the music of the secular dance with the central myth of Western European and American societies. Some Christians at youth clubs would not dance to the music of *Jesus Christ, Superstar* because, for them, the boundary between rock music with its sensuality, and religious rituals which do not allow sensual dancing in this form, was being confused too much. These two rock-musicals may mark either the beginning of the end of the Jesus myth as a sacred area in modern societies, that is the final move in the secularisation of Christianity, or the return of dancing and more spontaneous sensuality to the Christian religion. It is more likely they will not have that much influence either way; neither increasing secularisation of the Christian myth, nor reintroducing the dance and sensuality to Christianity. The split is too deep for these rock operas to overcome.

DANCE

The key area where church ritual has departed from other ritual actions is in dance. The sacred procession is one of the few examples of movement to rhythm left in the Christian Church in the West, and it is very basic to ritual in all denominations, both Protestant and Catholic. Many people receive a 'thrill' from seeing a Sunday School procession of Protestant denominations walking to the sound of music, usually from a brass band. There are a number of other moments in religious rituals where people move to music, which is the basic form of dance, for instance when the people go to the altar rail to receive communion and the choir are singing a hymn. Some churches have introduced a new ritual act during the offertory, where the congregation all walk to the steps of the sanctuary to put their money for the collection in a plate, during the singing of a hymn. This replaces the sidesmen who walk round to take the collection during the singing of a hymn. It is a more effective uniter of the congregation, more powerful as a symbol of people offering their whole selves, not just money, and it has more power to affect people's experience of the 'numinous' if it is done well, to the right music.

There is a dance round the altar during the rite of marriage in the Eastern Orthodox Church. However, the Christian Church has condemned dancing almost from its inception as a major organisation—St Basil did so (A.D. 344-407)—and certainly during the Middle Ages, when condemnation reached its peak. Dancing therefore occurred in secular settings, in special dance halls, at parties, and in the theatre. The separation of dancing from the Church's religious rituals has led to the whole sphere of arts and entertainment developing dance music and dancing to such an extent that it has become a major competitor with organised religion. This development has probably been much more significant in affecting church attendance than the growth of science as an alternative belief system, for the arts and entertainment involve the mind, the emotions and the body.[17]

The hostility between the Churches and dancing lies in the fact that dancing is sensual and erotic, in that it takes delight in the human body and displays it, such that both dancers themselves, and the audience, if there is one, may feel aroused and excited sensually by dance. As Geradus van der Leeuw pointed out in his *Sacred and Profane Beauty: The Holy in Art*:

> It is obvious that a view of life which shrinks from the body cannot stand for beautiful movement; that a religion which exalts virginity above all else must hate the enticements of the moving body; that the hope for release from the body through death expects no benefit from any expression of feeling, and certainly not from any expression of the holy, through dance.[18]

He goes on to make the point that a number of theologians now make, that this denigrating attitude towards the body is a 'mistaken' version of Christianity, for the body is 'good', according to the doctrine of the Creation and the Incarnation. Nevertheless, historic Christianity, as distinct from the views of modern Christian intellectuals, has had a profound influence on the cultures of Europe in the direction of distrust for the body and, therefore, of dancing.

The beauty of the human body has been expressed through the arts and entertainment, and to some extent through sport, although in the case of sport the aesthetic and erotic elements are kept to a minimum. In much modern art the human body has been lost in abstractions, although some sculpture, such as that of Henry Moore, has retained a sensual and human element. The one exception has been dance, which has gained enormously from the shift to abstract movements of the whole body during this century. This has affected popular dancing too, in that people more or less invent the movements they wish when dancing to modern rock music, as distinct from the carefully controlled steps of ballroom dancing.

Modern ballet and modern dance are now so closely related that old barriers between the types of music used for dance are being broken down. Alwin Nickolais composes his own electronic musical sounds for his dance company.[19] This is an increasingly used method, being less expensive than a live band or orchestra and better than recorded music because it is written with the dancers in mind. This sort of development begins to break down the gap between the audiences for classical ballet and pop music, such that the audiences at theatres, where the new type of dance companies appear, are mixed. Some people are part of the audience for classical ballet, whose interest is in dance as an art-form, others are more interested in pop art and new forms of theatre. Obviously there can be over-lap in that some people like classical ballet and pop music, nevertheless a new form of art-entertainment is emerging in the area of modern dance, which may develop its own special audience, but is at the moment fluid and socially more open and mixed than other theatre audiences usually are.[20]

The interest among some people, often under thirty years old, in Eastern religions can be seen in part to derive from the split in the West between religious ritual and the dance. Many of the new oriental cultic movements which have developed in the late 1960s and early seventies include dance as part of their method for gaining religious experiences and knowledge. This is true of many forms of Hinduism from India, where dance plays an integral part in many of the ritual events, such as feast days and initiation rites. Dance is found also in Sufism, a movement which has grown in popularity recently. Dance is part of the method for attaining 'fana', a condition of ecstasy and forgetfulness attained through deliberate practice, not drug induced.

AESTHETIC RITUAL IN THE WORKING CLASSES

People who earn their living by wage-labour within capitalist societies, such as Britain, are the classical type of working class in the Marxist and Weberian conceptual schemes. There is clearly some degree of differentiation among this group, based on earning capacity as well as on status-honour. There is a distinction between 'respectable' working-class people and 'non-respectable' working-class people, made at least by workers interviewed in an Anglican congregation in an outer London housing estate.[21] It is because it affects action towards both religion and aesthetic rituals that such a differentiation has to be noted for this section. For example, workers in Wales or Yorkshire who enjoy singing in male voice choirs such works as Handel's *Messiah* or various hymns and chorales, usually belong to the 'respectable' section of working-class communities. One factor affecting respectability turns on attitudes to, and use of, drink; the less respectable workers get drunk fairly frequently. The Temperance Movement's influence can still be seen, reinforced by Methodism and other religious groups, such as the Salvation Army.

Singing, like playing in brass bands, often was originally related to churches and chapels in these communities, but has usually become separated from these specifically religious organisations, as the group meeting to make music finds that this is a meaningful social group, which relates to aesthetic symbols, but primarily to religious experiences. Dennis Marsden has described the atmosphere of a brass band group very well in *Working Class Community*, by Brian Jackson:

In a time of extreme crisis, such as the Great Strike, they [brass bands] might emerge for a moment as a voice of protest and unity. They are one of the reserves of community. But in the normal tenor of life they are not so central to community as they may seem.[22]

The brass bands emerged in the way suggested during the protest against the Industrial Relations Bill in 1971, and in the miners' strike and the victory celebrations held for the miners in 1972.

Music brings the working class closest to aesthetic ritual of a middle-class type. This extends to pop music, and entertainments in the pub, the clubs and dance halls. Making and listening to music is the ideal-type form of aesthetic ritual, for groups meet to relate to a symbolism which has a unique aesthetic quality, as Susanne Langer has articulated in her work.[23] It can be related to political or religious ideas, but it retains a life of its own, independent of the content of any works associated with it. This aspect of music seems to be universally appreciated, with its own devotees and virtuosi in all social classes and ethnic groupings. There can be overlaps in the musical sub-cultures of the middle and working classes, as is the case in England with an oratorio like the *Messiah* or a modern pop musical like *Jesus Christ, Superstar*. There is the important difference that the former is much more based in the older generation's own culture, whereas the latter is, in part, commercially pushed. However, both works have been popular with some members of all classes and generations.

It is this potential capacity in music towards universality that means that it can lead to insights of a religious and political character, which stress equality, love and universal brotherhood of man. There are numerous examples of this, from Beethoven, in his Ninth Symphony, to Stockhausen's ideas and music, and in socialist hymns such as the 'Internationale', or the 'Red Flag'. Here, there is a relation between the forms of music, and its own unique method of communicating, based on melody and rhythm, and the content, in that it is being suggested that although music is a symbol system *sui generis*, if it carries a 'content' at all, then 'universalism' is suggested by music itself. In cases where the content is not universalistic it would be the case that the content has been made primary, and its origins lie outside music as such, as in many national anthems. This is only an hypothesis, but it would be worth further development in empirical studies.

Football is another working-class ritual. The civic ritual aspects have already been mentioned in the chapter on 'Nationalism and Civic Ritual'. There is, however, an aesthetic aspect to football, i.e. soccer, which is akin to dance. When a move is made gracefully by a group of players, or just one, there is an element of aesthetic experience for the players and for the audience.[24] It is akin to the circus, to acrobats, and to 'rough theatre' in which the actors use their bodies a great deal, and do not just portray a character. Gymnastics and athletics can have similar effects at times. And racing pigeons, dogs, horses, as well as humans, can all give aesthetic experience to their fans.

Aesthetic rituals must not be seen as a middle-class pheno-menon only. In England there are numerous examples which have been mentioned in which working-class people make their own aesthetic rituals. So do various ethnic minorities, especially the West Indians in England who have developed a distinctive music of their own—steel bands and 'reggae'. The blacks in America have developed a unique form in jazz, blues and 'soul' music. Just as a form, such as traditional and modern jazz, which was developed in a particular historical situation by an exploited group can have a universal significance for many other groups in different historical circumstances, so can some aesthetic forms developed by artists working for highly economi-cally privileged groups have a potentiality beyond those historical circumstances. This would be true of much European 'classical' music for example. To assert otherwise is to deny aesthetic symbols and rituals the unique, *sui generis*, characteristics asserted for them here. Middle-class people who pay little attention to jazz or other popular forms of music, and some left-wing groups who deny any aesthetic validity to, say, European classical music, opera and ballet, because of the nature of the class who originally supported the composers, singers and players of that music, are both narrowing the universal potential-ities of these aesthetic forms. Indeed they show no real concern for music as such, but only for music or other art forms when in the service of some set of values derived from elsewhere, such as their class, or racial position. This is to ignore a crucial potentiality of aesthetic symbols and rituals, especially those involving music, to unite people around experiences of a precious kind. It is to give up the great task of mankind—to find a way of being more unified, politically, economically, militarily, and also culturally—at a point in time when it is just beginning, and is just possible to envisage, given modern means of communication.[25]

Cinema is another form which may carry mythic material, and to this extent approaches being ritual action. Both middle- and working-class people attend cinemas, although increasingly there is an age factor at work; younger people attend cinemas, leaving their parents at home watching television. This way they escape from the surveillance of parents at home for a time and can dress up in fashionable clothes to 'go out' and make a special occasion.

The issues raised by cinema are vast, and need a separate study. Cinema is not a central form of ritual action for the purposes of this analysis, for it involves only very minimal body movement on the part of the audience, and there is no real contact between members of the audience of the kind that occurs in a theatre, because the absence of live actors means that there is no reflection of feelings going on between performers and audience. The mythic themes of the cinema are important, but belong more to the study of myth than of ritual. The Western film has been analysed to some degree as myth by, for example, Leslie Fielder.

Hollywood musicals have been examined to some extent by Peter Wollen, and Ivan Butler has examined the portrayal of biblical stories and witchcraft on the screen.[26] There are also numerous studies of particular directors' works.

CONCLUSION

In capitalist societies, and communist ones too, the arts as much as religion have to be developed within a given economic and political framework. This does not mean it could be otherwise, for any social structure will have influences on the rituals and symbols developed, the conditions under which people relate to them, and the meaning they have in their lives. An important way in which capitalist society has affected the development of the arts is through turning all the arts into a commodity to be bought and sold and invested in, such that profits can be made out of artistic activity of all kinds. Under the Welfare State capitalisms of Western Europe, the state and public authorities play a larger role in supporting the arts than they used to before the Second World War, and more than occurs in the United States.

The arts are not safe for any institution which seeks to avoid change, for they can challenge people to think about their lives and to alter them. Much art, therefore, which is supported by any institution or a political party like the Communist Party of the Soviet Union, will tend to be not too disruptive. Ways are found of controlling it by putting it in the category of 'great art', to be admired but not internalised and appreciated in a way which might alter people's lives towards a more spontaneous and creative way of being.

Creative arts are a threat to any group which seeks to rule others in a society or an organisation in an élitist, authoritarian, non-participative manner. This is because creativity, and creative responses to art, lead to a degree of spontaneity and creativeness which authoritarian structures cannot handle. The Churches, with bishops in their organisational structure, and those with an ascetic, puritanical ethic among the Protestant and non-conformist denominations, were not able to contain the popular arts, entertainment, nor 'élite' arts. Crucially, they could not contain the people who worked in these new areas, nor their followers and admirers. Ritual and symbolic needs were catered for in new, more spontaneous, physical and erotic forms, in the dance halls, theatres, pubs and music-halls.

Chapter Eight

Ritual, Social Change and Counter-Culture

The main process which has been analysed and described in the previous chapters concerns the increasing differentiation of the four main types of ritual action in modern industrial societies. There are complex social processes underlying this increasing differentiation of types of ritual in the main institutional areas of English society. The Church of England has been a national Church, providing rituals which reinforce nationalism. This is less necessary than it was, given the growth of television coverage of many 'nationalist' events which are not primarily religious, such as plays about the founding fathers of England and sporting events. Many within the Church, albeit a minority, want the Church to be less nationalistic than it has been. Thus, there is increasing pressure to differentiate religious and national political rituals, but it has by no means been fully worked through yet, and probably never will be. The Church's attitude to the body, sensuality and sexuality, has been, along with other Churches in Christain countries, very negative, with the result that aesthetic rituals have developed independently to express these aspects. Rituals concerned with the life cycle and life crises are still embedded in the ritual system of the Church of England, but here too there are attempts to differentiate membership and initiation into the Church as such, from merely being a member of an English parish by birth, but with no commitment to the Church.

This chapter is concerned with a different process to that of the differentiation of rituals, namely the attempts to reunify various areas of life into a less highly differentiated system. This process is what is termed here 'the creation of counter-culture'.[1] The counter-culture is a movement which stresses values and actions which lead to less specialisation and differentiation, and may lead to the development of communities in which work, family life, and symbolic, ritual, events are all experienced with the same, relatively small, number of people.[2] These communities are the most definite in their commitment to less differentiation in a society. They include religious communities, Christian, Sufi, Buddhist and Hindu, as well as artistic communities and political ones.[3] Apart from these there are also new types of action occurring in the theatre, in group psycho-therapy, in pop festivals and dances, in groups using cannabis and LSD, and in new forms of religious worship in the various world religions, all of which reintegrate ritual action with other experiences that had become more and more differentiated and split off from one another. So, for example, there is dance in various Western Hindu rituals and Sufi rituals; there may be something approaching worship in some dance-theatre, and group psycho-therapy links with some forms of new theatre, as well as dealing with problems of meaning, and providing a new ethic, especially in regard to personal relationships and sexuality.

The counter-culture is a term used for all of these attempts to break away from conventional forms of separation of spheres of living. This is a definition chosen specially for this analysis, and is not meant to be exhaustive of all that may be found among groups claiming themselves to be in some way against the prevailing culture, its values, symbols and rituals. Yet it does help define the sociologically relevant aspect of counter-culture, namely its attempts to reverse one of the central processes of modern societies, the splitting off from one another of various roles and life experiences.

The system of work and wage-labour, payment by the hour or week, is a central means of controlling people in capitalist societies as they are at present constructed and therefore, in America especially, the counter-culture has flourished among the affluent young, who are independent of the system of wage-labour to some degree. In Britain there is both a counter-culture among middle-class young, based on the universities, and one based on working-class communities, both of which share a value system which places emphasis on group pleasures rather than the values and psychological capacities of the world of work. It is in such groups that the reintegration of ritual with the rest of group life might potentially take place. Ritual action of the kind meant here can sustain and articulate forms of consciousness and their associated values and action, which are in tension with the dominant forms of social action in industrial society—namely technical, instrumental, calculative action.[4] The recent opposition of youth to technocratic culture has rarely been related to longer existing ritual actions in industrial societies, rituals which are more institutionalised, but do not necessarily always serve to maintain the *status quo*. Some opposition in the USSR, however, seems to be 'religious', in that young people become members of Orthodox congregations.

Some clergy and laity in the Churches, artists of all kinds, and part of their audiences, the drug-youth—oriental sub-culture, cultural minorities and ethnic minorities, and students; all these play a part in the counter-culture process. Jurgen Habermas writes that students have

a lack of understanding why despite the advanced stage of technological development the life of the individual is still determined by the dictates of professional careers, the ethics of status competition, and by values of possessive individualism and available substitute gratification; why the institutionalised struggle for existence, the *discipline of alienated labour, eradication of sensuality and aesthetic gratification are perpetuated* (italics mine R. B.).[5]

The estrangement of many students and others in the late 1960s and early seventies from highly formalised intellectual 'hard' sciences lies in this suspicion about the capacity of such knowledge to aid men in leading happier lives; it seems to increase mankind's problems as much as solving them. Hence, more practically oriented, experiential types of knowledge gain, in that they appear to offer more control over how the knowledge is used than highly abstract science. The faith that from abstract science, and its continued development, will flow more and more benefits, is questioned by more and more students. The answer is still positive for some—science is worth pursuing for its possible aid to men. For others the answer is 'No'.[6]

RITUAL AND SOCIAL CHANGE

Ritual action can have two sorts of consequences for the society in which it takes place: either it can provide a process whereby people become more attached to the basic way of life and values of the society, or to the major sub-groups within it of which the participants in ritual are a part;[7] or ritual can lead to people making new demands on the way of life in their society, and a desire to see change both in action and in the values the society pursues. Much social scientific work on ritual in simple societies has seen ritual as doing the former; there are fewer studies which seek to show the conditions under which change in action and in values can follow.[8] It is a major focus here to try to analyse the sociological conditions under which ritual action can lead to change in the values and way of life for significant groups in the society—significant not necessarily in a quantitative sense, but in terms of longer-term change. So although only a minority of youth are involved in the 'counter-culture', this group is nevertheless 'significant' in terms of the radically new values it has developed.

In discussing LSD and religious experience, Walter Pahnke writes:

If psychedelic drugs really can change people's goals, values, motivations and needs for achievement, the impact could be considerable on our society, in which there is so much stress on money, power and status. Less emphasis on these traditional goals, coupled with the availability of more leisure time, could alter our style of life. Some argue that such changes in moderation might be healthy, yet it is possible that widespread adoption of a radical change in outlook might be disastrous to a society that wants mainly to multiply its Gross National

Product and to compete successfully. Such issues need realistic and sensitive consideration.[9]

If one asks from where do new values come in society, and how do they emerge, then one can see the importance of both economic, material interests and the demands for these to be met, by, for instance, the working classes, and also what Weber called 'ideal' interests, that is interests deriving from the belief system of a group.[10] Ritual action has much of its importance in this second category—in that there is a complex connection between a belief system, values and ritual action. Ritual can have importance in rallying people to act in order to protect their economic interests, or their physical survival, in time of attack and war. Rituals certainly have this function in simple societies where life is much less differentiated than in industrial societies. This still continues in modern society—e.g. the political or trade union rally, meeting, demonstration or strike action. The latter is not only ritual, but it is in part. Men on strike develop their own symbols and rituals, such as songs, phrases used in speeches to rally the strikers, marches and banners with the symbols of the union on them. But deeper than this is the way in which participation in such an event as a demonstration or strike, or sit-in, or political rally leads to the experience of co-operation of men in a common cause, and sometimes the articulation of values of co-operation and good will to other people outside the group.

Ritual action is a crucial part of the process whereby any society maintains itself, and contains dissident elements within it. It is also a crucial area for the forwarding of liberation, for the building up of movements of people to change the society. In the area of ritual action is to be found a key expression of the struggle for human liberation, which goes on alongside and to some extent independent of the economic struggle. It is of great importance given a conception of human beings as needing symbolic meanings in their lives over and above, the economic material base, as Herbert Marcuse argues in talking about 'the new sensibility' among Western youth.[11] The economic, material struggle is basic—as Britain relearned in 1972, during the miners' strike and the industrial disruptions which followed. In addition to this there continues the struggle in the area of ritual action—whose meanings will predominate, whose way of feeling life will come through in the popular arts, and in religion?

Britain, like other industrial capitalist societies, is a society in which there is the continual possibility of a crisis in finance, commerce, and industry; and during such crises the re-opening of class conflicts on a deep scale are seen. When the capitalist economy works for periods of years without such deep crises, the society looks relatively cohesive, as in Britain from 1950 to about 1970. With the coming of the crises, the cohesion breaks down and varying degrees of depth conflicts emerge. The idea of a unified society, consensually governed by a body of law all accept, broke down in Northern Ireland and to some extent in England, Scotland and Wales in 1972. During such periods, people learn a great deal about the nature of society, and many of the attempts made to legitimate it break down and fail to work.[12] So the Christian Church services in Northern Ireland, which expressed the unity of Catholics and Protestants, failed to transfer into real political action because nationalist sentiments, disguised as in part religious, were stronger.

A view of social change must reflect assumptions about the nature of man as well as assumptions about the nature of society. Is any social change to be seen as a reflection of basic human propensities? Is man perfectable by changing societies, or will there always be violence and wars, misery and injustice? Does man's biological make-up set limits to his social possibilities? If so, what are these limits? These questions cannot be answered given present-day knowledge. Nevertheless, they need to be borne in mind in any discussion of social change, for it is always too easy to forget that they are not yet answered, and to build theories which may prove to be unwarranted and unreal, when we understand more about human biology and its relation to culture and social structures.[13]

For some purposes the work of Freud, and some of those who have developed his ideas, is extremely useful as a theory of human nature which is linked to social structure, to power and

26 Members of 'Hare Krishna' group, dancing and chanting in the West End, London, 1971.

27 People at a pop festival, 1972. It is in a group like this, sitting in a circle, that many people would smoke 'pot'.

28 Pop-singer. Pop and folk so often transmit counter-cultur values.
Singer—Raymond Froggatt.

29 Student demonstration, L don, 1969. Part of the polit counter-culture developed am students. Note the use of picture Marxist heroes, as symbols in procession.

WORKERS OF ALL COUNTRIES. UNITE !

authority, and to institutions such as the family, religion and the arts. Freud makes emotions central in his theory of man, and of the mind. Of the various feelings men experience, there seems to be one above all which helps us understand men's actions, their dreams and fantasies, and their ideas and thoughts —this is *desire*. 'If we take "desire" as the most suitably abstract of this series of terms, it is a Freudian axiom that the essence of man consists, not, as Descartes maintained, in thinking, but in desiring.'[14]

This view is further developed by Norman Brown in a way which is highly relevant to social change and ritual. In so far as ritual, as the term is used here, includes the arts and entertainment, the following quotation can be seen to have relevance to this analysis. '. . . if man's destiny is to change reality until it conforms to the pleasure-principle, and if man's fate is to fight for instinctual liberation, then art appears, in the words of Rilke, as the Weltanschauung of the last goal.'[15]

Here is where history has to be combined with the non-historical: man's basic symbols. To understand some ritual actions it is necessary to allow understanding to develop on two levels: one level within historical time, and the other in a more timeless way. These levels are similar to Levi-Strauss' use of diachronic and synchronic methods.[16]

The timeless level is the one dealt with more by depth psychology, psycho-analysis, and allied approaches; it is concerned with features of man's psychic life and his organic growth and decay which have faced all human beings in all historical periods, although experienced differently in various cultures. In spite of this cultural variety there has been found to be some similar themes in myths and religious rituals in a wide variety of settings and time periods. The work of Jung and his co-workers has illustrated this to a quite high degree, and, although it is different in approach, the work of Levi-Strauss has found structural relationships of this more timeless universal type. Researchers in the comparative history of religions have also noted similarities in world religions, around such themes as sacrifice and worship.

Sociology has a special opportunity to relate these two levels

M

together, and needs to develop some theoretical tools for this task. Social sciences at present tend to work on only one time level, for instance some sociology and anthropology of a functionalist type is ahistorical; social history rectifies this to some extent. In both these approaches, however, the psychic unconscious level has not been brought in. It is very difficult to relate the two levels in one and the same analysis, for the one way of looking at social action seems to make the other impossible at the same time. Looked at in one way the whole of a piece of social ritual action may seem to relate only to present and recent time, but the same data, or capta, can also appear under the other mode of analysis as part of timeless mythic reality. For example, a wedding is in part a ritual event in the lives of two people and two families which occurs at a specific time and place and is in this respect unique.[17] It may also be viewed as an example of more basic human issues of the relations between the sexes and the legitimate birth of children, using ritual actions which are often millennia old, indeed whose original meaning is lost to us now—e.g. giving a ring and wearing it on a special finger.

ALIENATION, WORK AND RITUAL

For Marx alienated labour is a means of physical existence: 'just as alienated labour transforms free and self-directed activity into a means, so it transforms the species life of man into a means of physical existence.'[18] Under the conditions prevailing in modern industrial society, especially those of capitalism in the latter half of the twentieth century, both work and aesthetic, religious and civic, rituals are performed under alienated conditions. Much of man's potential is expressed through religious ritual, political ritual and aesthetic rituals. Rituals are social, co-operative activities which express a kind of creativity, and which relate men to one another and to nature in a way which can provide a glimpse of non-alienated living. Ritual need not always be seen as reconciling men to their state of misery and lack of freedom under alienated conditions; it can keep alive new and fresh perspectives, innovative ways of relating to nature, self and others. It can inspire men to further creativity and new kinds of liberation. Thus there is no need to define ritual in terms of a behaviour carried out in accordance with unchanging rules, for there can be spontaneity and creativity within ritual, for instance, in aesthetic rituals where control and creativity do meet.[19]

It is also important to realise that ritual may involve what might appear to some as regression to earlier stages of mankind's development; for recovery of unconscious processes can appear like this to those who see it in progressivist terms. Marxism makes itself unnecessarily restrictive, if it leaves out the symbolic life of man. Psycho-analytic perspectives falsify man's life in society by ignoring and undervaluing the social and the historical.

Ritual action is very centrally tied in with experience of time. It is an attempt to hold time; to recreate important events; and even to live in a timeless world. Rituals aim to alter and conquer time. They do this by a period of what Mircea Eliade called 'concentrated time'—'. . . we must become aware of what it is in a modern existence that is still "mythical", and survives as such simply because this, too, is part and parcel of the human condition, in that it expresses the anxiety of man living in Time.'[20]

The activities of some Marxist groups come near to being ritual occasions to enact commitment to a myth, to alter time, to bring 'the day of renewal' nearer, if not indeed to experience it in the here and now. This is not to disvalue such occasions, for it can be argued that such groups as these are the main agents of social change in modern society.

Men seem to need to relate to the natural world in a way which is much richer, more meaningful on a psychic level, than that of instrumental work on nature as conducted in industrial society. Marx's notion of a 'sensuous' relationship with nature is nearer to what is meant here than the usual puritanised conception of our society:

Man appropriates his manifold being in an all-inclusive way, and thus as a whole man. All his human ways of relating himself to the world—seeing, hearing, smelling, tasting, touching, thinking, observing, feeling, desiring, acting, loving—in short all the organs of his individuality, are social in form in their objective action (their action in relation to the object) the appropriation of this object, the appropriation of human reality.[21]

ROLE DIFFERENTIATION AND SPECIALISTS IN RITUAL ACTION

Modern industrial societies have been developing specialised roles and organisations for more and more specific tasks and social activities. It is this process of differentiation which has led to the specialised ritual systems of religious organisations, artistic and entertainment organisations and of political parties and movements. This has resulted in a degree of social isolation for the various specialists, especially clergy and artists of all kinds. They have become cut off from the everyday experience of the people with whom they are trying to communicate, and have often found communication difficult. This is the case with clergy whose understanding of Christianity is often more 'liberal' and open than is the case with their congregations. Many artists find they can easily become too isolated, their work is not related to everyday life but treated as special, set apart—sacred.[22] This has led some to question the whole idea of art as concerned with 'beauty' or aesthetics. For example, the sculptor Robert Morris declared: 'The undersigned, Robert Morris, being the maker of the metal construction entitled Litanies . . . hereby withdraws from said construction all aesthetic quality and content and declares that from the date hereof said construction has no such quality and content.'[23]

Many specialists in religious organisations and in the arts feel that the Church, or the arts, should be more related to social reality than they are at present. Yet for many of the congregations and audiences this view is often difficult to understand since they are seeking relief and solace in the rituals of the Church, or from the arts. The tensions arise from the fact that the specialists' whole lives are spent concerned with the rituals and symbols of religion and/or the arts. It is really *their lives* that are unrelated to everyday living by virtue of their specialised role in the division of labour in industrial societies. Some clergy have come to realise this, and seek to be employed in the ordinary, profane, work world. If they still seek to show how the sacred and its values can be used in such situations as industry, they may find great difficulties, because the way organisations operate is such that they are outside the ethical surveillance of any religion. They work according to their own logic of rational, efficient administration, involving making profits, being competitive, and running smoothly. In any case such a solution involves heavy emphasis on the ethical content of a religion, rather than its ritual and symbolic content. For artists, such a solution is very difficult. They may work in a school, a mental hospital, or prison and thus feel they have become more relevant than would otherwise be the case. But they too are essentially a peripheral addition, able, like clergy, to slightly humanise some situations from time to time. The organisation continues to work basically according to its own values.

Recently there have been completely different types of solution to these problems of the over-specialisation of the arts and religion, and the difficulty of finding either art of religion relevant to modern life. These attempts have occurred in what has been termed the 'counter-culture', or the 'alternative society'. This is difficult to fully define, or identify empirically, with clear-cut boundaries. Rather than it being an empirical social group, like the Jews for example, it is preferable for sociological purposes to see it as a social process, in which many people may be involved from time to time. There may be some who are identifiable as being in an alternative societal group for nearly their whole lives, such as those who join a religious community. Other people may support such groups with money, either in the form of gifts, or in purchasing goods made by such communities; they may use the communities for a retreat, or for meditation; and they may see themselves as being in broad sympathy with the values and way of life of such communities. The same can be true of groups which are devoted to the arts. There are a number of theatre groups which live almost as complete communities, for at least a number of years, although they do not tend to last as long as religious communities. For example, the group around Jerzy Grotowski in Poland live as a community and produce theatre, or ceremony, for those who wish to assist. 'Grotowski makes poverty an ideal; his actors have given up everything except their own bodies; they have the human instrument and limitless time—no wonder they feel the richest theatre in the world.'[24]

Time is central to the problem. The reason specialists in the arts and in religion arise is so that there will be some people who have the time, free from profane activities, to devote their lives to develop the beliefs, values and rituals of society. The specialists that developed under capitalism have become highly individualised, particularly in the arts and entertainment. They have spent hours and hours of their time rehearsing, composing, creating, working at their art, and live by selling the product of this time, which may be a product of their artistic skill, as an *individual*. Theatre comes closest to being a group activity, but even here, until very recently, there was always a 'star' performer, whose salary would be higher than the other actors. Group theatre overcomes this through sharing, and through living more simply. It therefore comes closest to the religious community in the way it solves the economic problem of those who wish to specialise, in depth, in self-exploration, and exploration of others, through ritual and symbol. It is a form of collective poverty which works successfully, at least for a time. It may be that some religious communities are more stable over time by requiring celibacy. Sexuality can be a disturbing element in a small community unless socially controlled in some mutually agreed way. There are religious communities which have lasted for centuries which do allow marriage, but they tend too to be very puritanical about sexuality in general, using it only for procreation, e.g. the Mormons.[25]

Community living avoids the problems which are produced for the individual artistic specialist, and for the clergyman or dedicated lay person in a religion. The symbols and rituals are related to the whole of life in the group. The small size of the group allows for meetings in depth between people over long periods of time; the singing together, dancing, making things, worshipping, becomes much more meaningful for everyone involved than can ever be the case in large, complex industrial societies, where congregations and audiences do not know one another in any depth.

Yet they can become cut-off and élitist; this time it is a group, not an individual, which has the problem of how to relate to the rest of the society. Religious communities have been of two types: some have done good works such as teaching or nursing, while others have been contemplative orders only. (Tax laws and anti-religious laws can affect the latter adversely, if they classify contemplative orders as 'non-charitable', or as 'socially non-useful', parasitic organisations.) Any community of the kind described above, which is in some ways an alternative society, may seek to relate to the outside world by doing good works. This is the case with political communes of the kind which have arisen in West Germany, England and America. These communes are composed of people who have chosen to withdraw from the ordinary society in order to have time to be more political, and to avoid being profaned by too much contact with the corrupt organisations and occupations of modern post-war capitalism. Their problems arise because they typically have no positive ways of handling the community's internal meaning problems, and tensions among members. They exist primarily as a way of aiding the members to be politically active on the rest of society; the interest in self-exploration and symbols and rituals of the religious and artistic communities can appear to the politicos to be a form of bourgeois indulgence. Yet it is being asserted here, on the basis of sparse evidence admittedly, that such political communes are unviable for long, unless they develop a positive interest in their commune as a way of life in itself. If they do this, then some kind of collective ritual and symbol system will emerge to celebrate joyful events, to mourn sorrowful events, and to recommit the members to the community's way of life.

Some communes have tried to use methods derived from psycho-analytic ideas, especially those concerned with group processes. There are certainly many individuals from the middle classes of modern capitalist societies who also attend various types of group-therapy sessions, for a variety of reasons.[26] Some attend to improve their capacity at work to manage people, and improve human relations in work organisations. Others go on medical advice, because perhaps therapy would be too expensive. Others go to help themselves enjoy life more. An example of the latter, which is part of 'the alternative society' in its values, is 'Quaesitor' in London. Here, a variety of techniques are used such as Encounter Groups, and methods derived from Gestalt therapy, Reichian body therapy, and the existentialist therapy of Laing.[27] These methods can be used by groups which live as communities, but there is little or no systematic research on the success of this that exists in English. 'Quaesitor' have developed events in which music, dance, drama, ritual are used to create a social occasion which is an undifferentiated form of religious—civic—aesthetic—body ritual. The event itself is seen as part of a political process of change away from the culture of advanced capitalist society which emphasises work, activism, competitiveness, towards a culture which stresses '*being*' rather than '*doing*', co-operation with others, and enjoyment in the present, rather than post-poning pleasures till they can be afforded.

Groups and communes which use drugs such as LSD and cannabis also develop such ritual occasions, and are based on values similar to those mentioned above. They are part of what Jock Young, following Matza and Sykes, calls *subterranean values*. These are short-term hedonism, spontaneity, ego-expressivity, autonomy, excitement and new experience activi-ties as ends in themselves, disdain for work. Activities such as dancing, playing music, acting, meditating, singing, even worshipping become central ritual events in such groups and communities.[28]

The process which has been called above that of making a counter-culture, or alternative society, reverses the basic assumption made by the main conventional society, and shared by many sociologists, especially Talcott Parsons, that ever-increasing differentiation of roles and organisations is both inevitable and desirable.[29] The counter-culture is a process in which areas of experience which have become separated one from another are being *reunited*. In place of differentiation and separation there is reunification. Art, religion, politics and life-cycle events are being brought together again in rituals within communities. The highly differentiated ritual system of the main society continues, and in some cases in the arts reaches new peaks of articulation and expression. So it must not be thought that the process of the counter-culture is replacing the basic process of specialisation and differentiation in the ritual system of industrial society. It has arisen in addition to it, and in some cases articulated ideologies against the main society. Both are typical modern processes; they are developing as two opposed ways of life in industrial society. Yet the counter-culture cannot escape being related to the main culture and society, if only to pick up those who can stand the pressures of the main society's values and way of life no longer. The full members of alternative societies (the plural seems more realistic than the singular, for there are a number of groups involved) are deviants and may under certain circumstances contribute to socio-cultural change.

What are these circumstances? There are a number of possibilities, leaving aside that of a revolution which led to socialism! Firstly, the counter-culture values can affect young people through the influence of pop songs and drug groups. The more creative members of the pop music world reflect values which are part of the counter-cultural 'subterranean' system. In part this is through the simple existence of music on such a large scale, and the growing amount of time spent listening and playing it by many young people now, compared with a generation ago. Music can become more important an activity to some young people than education and work, and it does offer a possible way of life for those who are good enough, or in the right place at the right time. Young people who take drugs are likely to do so in a group where one of the members may have read some of the drug literature which contains subterranean values, and this helps define the situation and formulate values.[30]

Secondly, the counter-culture's negative attitude to organised work as it exists in capitalist societies, although not to *creative activity* people want to do, could be of real significance in adapting young people and others to the acceptance of unemployment in technologically advanced societies. Unemployment is still an economic disaster for many people, and as such should and will be fought. But voluntary unemployment is growing among the young of all social classes and this could be a fruitful development if only the Welfare State would accept it as a potentially positive development instead of being negative in both social and monetary terms to such people.[31]

Third, many younger teachers in colleges, universities, and schools hold values which are in large part akin to those of the counter-culture, although they have compromised by having a job in the system. Nevertheless, they can be of some influence in both seeking to change educational organisations from being authoritarian in structure, competitive and often boring for the pupils and students, and in transmitting values through their attitudes to living to the young people they meet. Pupils and students can pick up the attitudes of their teachers, without the teachers revealing them in lessons or classes in a direct way.

Fourth, the counter-culture has a more accepting attitude towards death, and is more aware of its tragic nature, and man's need to come to terms with it from very early in life. It is not swept away and ignored, or carefully concealed and covered up as in the main public culture of modern industrial society. This has not so far, done much to affect old people or people approaching retirement, but it may be that nothing will occur at this stage of the life cycle until the present generation under thirty reaches this stage itself—then it will be possible to see how far there has been a real change in cultural attitudes here. It may well be that those who sustain their commitment to counter-culture values through most of their lives will find retirement a non-event; it may not even happen to many, and dying will be an event which can be prepared for in a group.[32]

Fifth, there are contributions the counter-culture already makes, and can continue to do, towards human sexuality—what it is, how it is to be lived, its potentialities and joys, as well as dangers. Already it has altered attitudes among many groups towards male and female homosexuality, transvestitism, and other deviants, leading to less problems for those who enact these forms of sexual behaviour. The problems of secrecy, social isolation, guilt, self-punitiveness are removed or considerably lessened for people in the counter-culture groups such as Gay Liberation Front. The problem of sex roles is also made more manageable, either through acceptance of child-rearing by girls in some agricultural communes as natural and rewarding, or through acceptance of men and women as equals, and similar in their capacities. It is the tolerance of variety which is potentially important in the counter-culture: some women can be mothers if they choose, others not; just as some men can live with other men if they wish, or be fathers of large families.[33]

If there ever is a socialist revolution in Western societies, then the counter-culture's contributions in the above areas would still continue and be important in aiding people to adapt to the changed conditions. They could well find that they have the task of keeping the socialist regime human; for example, by allowing some people to choose to live in communities and not have to do work for the benefit of the State, decided for them by State bureaucrats. Something of the importance of the counter-culture's contribution can be seen by looking at such groups in Eastern Europe,[34] but it should be remembered that these societies are not socialist in the sense that America or France or Britain would be if these ever had democratic socialist revolutions, or evolved into socialism through an economic crisis producing a socialist majority in Parliament. The experience of some people in the counter-culture in the Soviet Union and Eastern Europe shows that under such regimes counter-culture groups need to be protected from interference by State officials, just as in the West they need protection from reactionary elements who would even kill some of them. The counter-culture is certainly a process which is by no means compatible with much that existing socialist societies are doing, for in many ways they share fundamental assumptions about work, technology, and authoritarianism in many organisations with the Western societies. Chinese experience is difficult to evaluate, for the Red Guards do not seem to have been all that similar to the counter-culture of Western capitalist societies, or Eastern European ones.[35] They were more political than the movements in the West, less interested in values, states of consciousness and religions, than the counter-culture of capitalism.

CONCLUSION

The discussion has been concerned with analysing the role of counter-cultural groups in capitalist society, especially those concerned with religious rituals and the arts. Some suggestions have been made about the ways in which they are contributing to socio-cultural change in such societies, and it has been shown that they are concerned above all with reuniting areas of human living and experience which have become too separate for their views of life to be realisable in industrial societies, perhaps socialist ones as well as capitalist ones, at least in Europe. There is here a problem, for many people in the counter-culture are products of the differentiated society and the wealth it has produced. For some the tension is too much, and so they become dedicated to poverty as one way of resolving this. Other people are less consistent and both accept parts of the counter-culture's values and symbols, and may attend its rituals, whether in the form of meditation, retreats, theatre events or therapies, yet they remain in the world and its occupational structure. There develops a tension between what Max Weber termed inner-worldly mysticism, that is seeking mystic states, *union with* the holy, while remaining in the world, and other-worldly mysticism, that is seeking union with the holy, contemplation, living outside of the world's ordinary occupations and ways of living.[36] Both these types of mysticism are, however, distinct from the asceticism of some aspects of Christianity and modern capitalist culture, which seek *mastery over* self or the natural world, or both, rather than *harmony with* nature, self and others.[37]

References

INTRODUCTION

1. For example, M. Douglas *Purity and Danger. An Analysis of Concepts of Pollution and Taboo* (Routledge and Kegan Paul, London 1966). Discusses health, dirt, bodies, dress, etc.
and
E. Leach, 'Anthropological Aspects of Language: Animal Categories and Verbal Usage', in E. H. Lenneberg (ed.) *New Directions in the Study of Language* (Massachusetts Institute of Technology Press, 1964) pp. 23-63. Also reprinted in P. Maranda (ed.) *Mythology* (Penguin Books, Harmondsworth 1972).

2. Max Gluckman *Essays on the Ritual of Social Relations* (Manchester University Press, 1962).
See also E. Leach, 'Ritual' in *International Encyclopaedia of the Social Sciences*.

3. D. Martin *A Sociology of English Religion* (Heinemann, London 1967).
B. Wilson *Religion in Secular Society* (C. A. Watts, London 1966).

4. See Bruyn *The Human Perspective in Sociology* (Prentice-Hall, Englewood Cliffs 1966).
B. Glaser and A. Strauss *The Discovery of Grounded Theory* (Weidenfeld & Nicolson, London 1968).
A. Cicourel *Method and Measurement in Sociology* (Free Press, Glencoe, New York 1964).

5. See M. W. Riley *Sociological Research* vol. 1 (Harcourt, Brace & World Inc., New York 1963) see Unit Two.

CHAPTER ONE

1. C. Wright Mills *The Sociological Imagination* (Penguin, Harmondsworth 1970) p. 37. This particular writer is chosen because he is a key figure in the development of New Left sociology, which in so many ways is important for this analysis. Yet it has this serious blind spot towards ritual and symbols.

2. See D. Martin *A Sociology of English Religion* (Heinemann, London 1967).
B. Wilson *Religion in Secular Society* (C. A. Watts, London 1966).
B. Martin, 'Comments on some Gallup Poll Statistics' in *A Sociological Yearbook of Religion in Britain* no. 1 (S.C.M. Press, London 1968).
Also important is: A. MacIntyre *Secularisation and Moral Change* (Oxford University Press, 1967).

3. Max Weber *The Sociology of Religion* (J. C. B. Mohr (Paul Seibeck), Germany 1922. Published in Great Britain 1965 by Methuen).

4. C. Jung *Modern Man in Search of a Soul* (Routledge and Kegan Paul, London 1933, reprinted 1966).

5. For instance this is true of what is in many ways the best substantial summary book on sociology of religion (in 1971), namely J. M. Yinger *The Scientific Study of Religion* (The Macmillan Company, New York; Collier-Macmillan, London 1970).

6. R. Otto *The Idea of the Holy* (Oxford University Press, 1923; Pelican Books, Harmondsworth 1959). This book is central to the view of religion developed here.

7. See S. Langer *Philosophy in a New Key* (Mentor Books, New York 1942, 1951) p. 45.

8. D. Morris *The Naked Ape* (Jonathan Cape, London 1967).
J. Lewis and B. Towers *Naked Ape or Homo Sapiens?* (Garnstone Press, London, second edition 1972).

9. Marxism in some of its forms is of this kind, as is much of the thought of Teilhard de Chardin, e.g. T. de Chardin *The Phenomenon of Man* (Collins, London 1959).
Also: various contributors *Evolution, Marxism and Christianity* (Garnstone Press, London 1967).

10. Christian sociology may be either demographic research, or social philosophy as with M. Reckitt *Faith and Society* (Longmans, Green, London 1932).

11. See O. Klapp *Collective Search for Identity* (Holt, Rinehart & Winston, U.S.A. 1969).

12. Otto, op. cit. (note 6).

13. For example, T. Luckmann *The Invisible Religion* (Collier-Macmillan, London 1971).
M. Spiro, 'Religion: Problems of Definition and Explanation' in M. Barton (ed.) *Anthropological Approaches to the Study of Religion* (Tavistock, London 1966) pp. 85-126.

14. A useful secondary source here is E. Pivcevic *Husserl and Phenomenology* (Hutchinson, London 1970).

15. D. Caute *The Illusion* (André Deutsch, London 1971). This book contains a lively discussion on the tensions between Marxism and Modernism in the arts; David Caute argues for socialists to take Modernism seriously, and not to insist on social realism and naturalism in the arts.

16. E. Durkheim *The Elementary Forms of the Religious Life* (Collier Books, New York 1961) p. 257.

17. P. Rieff *Freud. The Mind of the Moralist* (Victor Gollancz, London 1960; Methuen, University Paperbacks, 1965).

18. S. Freud's work on religion is to be found in *The Future of an Illusion*, 1928 and 1962; *Moses and Monotheism*; *Totem and Taboo*, and in *Civilisation and its Discontents* (The Hogarth Press and the Institute of Psycho-Analysis, London).

19. S. Freud *Obsessive Actions and Religious Practices* (Paper in the Collected Papers, Hogarth Press, London 1907).

20. Jung, op. cit. (note 4), pp. 264 and 260.

21. C. G. Jung *Man and His Symbols* (Aldus Books, London 1964).

22. There are still suspicions about the concept of the 'unconscious' among some social scientists. For a balanced assessment of the concept from the point of view of a linguistic philosopher, see A. MacIntyre *The Unconscious* (Routledge & Kegan Paul, London 1958).

23. J. P. Sartre *The Problem of Method* (Alfred A. Knopf, U.S.A.; Methuen, London 1963).

24. C. Levi-Strauss, *Totemism* (English translation copyright Beacon Press, 1963; Pelican Books, Harmondsworth 1969) p. 142.

25. ibid. p. 141.

26. D. Wrong, 'The Pitfalls of Social Reductionism', 'The Over-Socialised Conception of Man in Modern Sociology', *American Sociological Review*, vol. 26, 1961, pp. 183-93.

27. C. Levi-Strauss *The Savage Mind* (Weidenfeld & Nicolson, London 1966).

28. J. Piaget *Structuralism* (Routledge & Kegan Paul, London 1971; *Le Structuralisme*, Presses Universitaires de France, 1968).

29. See K. Marx and F. Engels *On Religion* (Lawrence & Wishart, London 1955).

See also J. Klugmann (ed.) *Dialogue of Marxism and Christianity* (Lawrence & Wishart, London 1968).

Also R. Garaudy *From Anathema to Dialogue* (Collins, London 1967)

30. Max Weber *The Methodology of the Social Sciences* (Free Press, Glencoe, New York 1949).

Max Weber, 'Science as a Vocation' in H. Gerth & C. Wright Mills (eds.) *From Max Weber: Essays in Sociology* (Oxford University Press, New York; Routledge & Kegan Paul, London 1946).

31. Max Weber *The Protestant Ethic and the Spirit of Capitalism* (Allen & Unwin, London 1930).

CHAPTER TWO

1. For material on secularisation, see Chapter One, Note 2.

Also D. Martin *The Religious and the Secular* (Routledge & Kegan Paul, London 1970).

2. M. Douglas, 'Heathen Darkness, Modern Piety' in *New Society*, 12 March 1970.

M. Douglas *Purity and Danger* (Routledge & Kegan Paul, London 1966; Pelican Books, Harmondsworth 1970).

3. This is beginning to change in some middle-class congregations in America, according to H. Cox *The Feast of Fools* (Harvard University Press, U.S.A. 1969). The first Christians danced, but St Basil (344-407), Bishop of Caesarea, was against it, and it disappeared, and was finally abolished in the Church almost completely in 1298.

4. See for example V. Turner's contribution to 'Forms of Symbolic Action' in *Proceedings of the American Ethnological Society*, 1969, Annual Spring Meeting (University of Washington Press, Seattle and London) pp. 3-25.

Also J. Huxley, 'A Discussion on Ritualisation of Behaviour in Animals and Man' in *Philosophical Transactions of Royal Society of London* Series B Biological Sciences, no. 772, vol. 251, 1966.

5. S. Langer *Philosophy in a New Key* (Harvard University Press, U.S.A. 1942).

6. See T. Roszak *The Making of a Counter Culture* (Faber, London 1970).

7. See report in *The Guardian*, 11 September 1971.

8. See for example D. R. Mace *The Christian Response to the Sexual Revolution* (Lutterworth Press, London 1971).

9. Max Gluckman *Essays on the Ritual of Social Relations* (Manchester University Press 1962). Gluckman's essay 'Les Rites de Passage'.

10. Cf. J. Goody, 'Religion and Ritual; The Definitional Problem', *British Journal of Sociology*, vol. XII, 1961, pp. 142-64. Goody defines ritual, following

Nadel, as 'Rigid acts of any kind'—this is a behavioural approach, and ignores the crucial symbolic element in ritual as defined here.

11. Gluckman, op. cit. (note 9) pp. 21-2.

12. Many recent writers have seen this feature as both central and unproblematic. See, for instance, M. Spiro, op. cit. (Chapter One, note 13). R. Robertson *The Sociological Interpretation of Religion* (Basil Blackwell, Oxford 1970).

13. T. Parsons *Societies. Comparative and Evolutionary Perspectives.* (Prentice Hall, U.S.A. 1966) chapter 2.

14. T. Parsons *The Social System* (Routledge & Kegan Paul, London 1951) chapter 9.

15. J. Israel *Alienation. From Marx to Modern Sociology* (Allyn and Bacon Inc., Boston, U.S.A. 1971) p. 111.

16. Roszak, op. cit. (note 6) p. 76.

17. L. Feuer *The Scientific Intellectual* (Basic Books, New York and London 1963) pp. 18-19.

18. Langer, op. cit. (note 5) p. 89, Mentor paperback edition.

19. ibid., p. 52.

20. M. Hollis, 'Reason and Ritual' in B. Wilson (ed.) *Rationality* (Basil Blackwell, Oxford 1970) p. 235.

21. E. Fromm *Psycho-Analysis and Religion* (Yale University Press, U.S.A. 1950) p. 105 of 1967 Bantam Books edition.

22. B. Wilson *Sects and Society* (Heinemann, London 1961).
   T. O'Dea *The Mormons* (University of Chicago, U.S.A. 1957).

23. D. Martin *The Religious and the Secular* (Routledge & Kegan Paul, London 1969).

24. A. Lowen *The Betrayal of the Body* (Collier-Macmillan, N.Y. 1967) p. 258.

25. I. C. Jarvie and J. Agassi, 'The Problem of the Rationality of Magic', *British Journal of Sociology*, vol. XVIII, 1967, pp. 55-74.

26. A. MacIntyre *Against the Self Images of the Age* (Duckworth, London 1971). See especially chapters 1, 13, and 21.

27. See for example how Max Gluckman handles rites of reversal and conflict in terms of their function for maintaining the 'established order', in his *Custom and Conflict in Africa* (Basil Blackwell, Oxford 1970) chapter 5 'Licence in Ritual'.

28. See for example the analysis of the Coronation in Britain by E. Shils and M. Young, 'The Meaning of the Coronation' in *Sociological Review*, vol. 1, 1953.

29. See J. Rex *Key Problems of Sociological Theory* (Routledge & Kegan Paul, London 1961).
   Also P. Cohen *Modern Social Theory* (Heinemann, London 1968).

30. Max Weber *The Sociology of Religion* (J. C. B. Mohr (Paul Siebeck), Germany 1922. Published in Great Britain 1965 by Methuen) chapter 9.
   P. Berger *The Social Reality of Religion* (Faber, London 1969) chapter 3.

31. Quoted in G. Woodcock *Anarchism* (The World Publishing Company, U.S.A. 1962; Pelican Books, Harmondsworth 1963) p. 179.

32. This view of Reason as linked with feeling follows ideas found in A. N. Whitehead *Modes of Thought* (Cambridge University Press, 1956). Also his *Adventures of Ideas* (Cambridge University Press, 1933 and 1961). Also S. Langer's work, especially in *Philosophy in a New Key* (see note 5).

33. T. Parsons and E. Shils *Towards a General Theory of Action* (Harvard University Press, U.S.A. 1951).

34. See G. Murray *Five Stages of Greek Religion* (Oxford University Press, 1925).

35. A. F. C. Wallace *Religion: An Anthropological View* (Random House, New York 1966) p. 106.

36. Wallace, op. cit., p. 104.

37. E. Pivcevic *Husserl and Phenomenology* (Hutchinson, London 1970). Husserl's phenomenology is by no means supportive of the so-called phenomenological school in recent sociology. Phenomenology is a position within philosophy of sociology, not a substantive theory within sociology itself, as this latter school seems to treat it. It is as a philosophical base for sociology, as an alternative to that of positivism, that it is being used in this book.

38. See Chapter Five on 'Nationalism and Civic Ritual 'in this book, for a fuller discussion of the Report of the Archbishop's Commission, *Church and State* (Church Information Office, London 1970).

39. Wallace, op. cit. (note 35) p. 70.

40. J. Fichter *Social Relations in the Urban Parish* (University of Chicago, U.S.A. 1954). Contains excellent discussion of problems in conceptualising boundaries of an urban congregation.

41. E. Durkheim *The Division of Labour in Society* (Macmillan Co., U.S.A. 1933) pp. 169 and 172 in Free Press, Glencoe, paperback edition, 1964.

42. L. F. Schnore, 'Community' in N. Smelser (ed.) *Sociology* (John Wiley & Sons, N.Y. 1967) p. 95.

43. F. Tonnies *Community and Society* (trans. C. Loomis) (Harper Torchbook, New York 1963).

44. Relevant here is M. Stacey, 'The Myth of Community Studies', *British Journal of Sociology*, vol. XX, 1969, pp. 134-47.

45. See R. Nisbet *The Sociological Tradition* (Basic Books Inc., U.S.A. 1966; Heinemann, London 1967) p. 80.

46. M. Buber *I and Thou*, 1937 (new translation by W. Kaufmann, 1970: C. Scribner's Sons, U.S.A. and T. & T. Clark, Edinburgh).

47. Nisbet, op. cit. (note 45).

48. For example, S. H. Foulkes and E. J. Anthony *Group Psychotherapy* (Penguin Books, Harmondsworth 1957 and 1965).

W. R. Bion *Experiences in Groups* (Tavistock Publications, London 1961).

J. Klein *Working with Groups* (Hutchinson, London 1961 and 1963).

49. *The Rite*, directed by I. Bergmann, 1969.

50. A. Etzioni *A Comparative Analysis of Complex Organisations* (The Free Press of Glencoe, Inc., New York 1961).

CHAPTER THREE

1. See R. J. Bocock, 'Ritual: Civic and Religious' in *British Journal of Sociology*, vol. XXI, 1970, pp. 285-97. The first section of this chapter is a shortened version of this article.

2. R. Otto *The Idea of the Holy* (first published 1917; English translation Oxford University Press, 1923; paperback edition, Pelican Books, Harmondsworth 1959).

3. E. Durkheim *The Elementary Forms of the Religious Life* (Collier Books by arrangement with the Free Press, New York 1961).

N

4. E. Underhill *Worship* (Nisbet, London 1938 and 1958).

5. Term used by Durkheim, op. cit. (note 3).

6. See T. O'Dea, 'Five Dilemmas in the Institutionalisation of Religion' in *Journal for the Scientific Study of Religion*, vol. 1, 1961, pp. 32-9. Reprinted in T. O'Dea *Sociology and the Study of Religion* (Basic Books, New York/London 1970).

7. T. Parsons *The Social System* (Routledge & Kegan Paul, London 1951) chapter 9, p. 397.

8. Parsons, op. cit.

9. In the book the terms 'Anglican Catholic' and 'Anglo-Catholic' refer to the same movement in the Anglican Church. The phrase used depends on the context. 'Anglo-Catholic' is now somewhat archaic, 'Anglican Catholic' being preferred by many, both in England and elsewhere, because it is less English in its connotation. Anglican Catholics are to be found in small but significant groups throughout the world.

10. See for example a pamphlet by K. M. Ross, 'What it means to be Catholic' (All Saints Booklets, no. 11, London).

11. M. Weber *The Protestant Ethic and the Spirit of Capitalism* (Allen & Unwin, London 1930 and 1962).

12. See O. Chadwick *The Mind of the Oxford Movement* (A. & C. Black, London 1960).

13. M. Douglas *Natural Symbols* (Barrie & Rockcliff: The Cresset Press, London 1970) see especially p. 42.

14. P. Worsley *The Trumpet shall Sound* (MacGibbon & Kee, London 1957). See Appendix to Paladin edition (Granada Publishing, London 1970) pp. 310-11.

15. B. Wilson *Religion in Secular Society* (C. A. Watts, London 1966) especially chapter 1. Quotation from Introduction, p. xi.

16. Wilson, op. cit., p. 2.

17. D. Martin *A Sociology of English Religion* (Heinemann, London 1967) p. 51.

18. T. Parsons, 'Christianity and Modern Industrial Society' in E. Tiryakian *Sociological Theory, Values, and Sociocultural Change* (Free Press of Glencoe, New York 1963).

19. Parsons, 'Christianity and Modern Industrial Society', op. cit.

CHAPTER FOUR

1. See I. Clutterbuck *What's happening to Our Discipline* (Church Union, Church Literature Association, London—no date, but late 1960s).

2. For this term see M. Weber *The Sociology of Religion* (Methuen, London 1965) chapters II and X.

3. E. Durkheim *The Elementary Forms of the Religious Life* (Collier Books, by arrangement with Free Press, New York 1961) book 1, chapter 1, section 3.

4. ibid., section 4.

5. J. A. Robinson *Christian Freedom in a Permissive Society* (S.C.M. Press, London 1970) p. 162 of paperback edition.

6. T. O'Dea *Sociology of Religion* (Prentice Hall, Englewood Cliffs, New Jersey 1966) quotation p. 21.

7. See T. Parsons *The Structure of Social Action* (Free Press of Glencoe, New York 1937) chapter XVII, section IV on Max Weber, 'Ritual', pp. 673-7 of the 1964 printing.

See also R. Nisbet *The Sociological Tradition* (Heinemann, London 1967) chapter 6.

8. Max Weber *The Sociology of Religion* (1922, German edition; 1963, Beacon Press; 1965 Methuen, London).

9. J. Wach *Sociology of Religion* (University of Chicago Press, 1944).

10. See R. J. Bocock, 'Anglo-Catholic Socialism: A Study of a Protest Movement within a Church' in *Social Compass*, vol. XX, 1973.

11. See, for example, D. B. Clark *Survey of Anglicans and Methodists in Four Towns* (Epworth Press, London 1965) and R. Frankenberg *Village on the Border* (Routledge & Kegan Paul, London 1957).

12. Dom Gregory Dix *The Shape of the Liturgy* (A. & C. Black, London 1945) p. 744.

13. Durkheim, op. cit. (note 3) book 3, chapter 2, section 4.

14. ibid., book 3, chapter 4.

15. See, for example, M. Reynolds *Martyr of Ritualism* (Faber, London 1965). About the trials of Fr MacKonochie of St Albans, Holborn, London, in the 1860s.

16. See quotation from Durkheim, p. 61 of this book.

17. A. Watts *Myth and Ritual in Christianity* (Beacon Press, U.S.A. 1968). This is an interesting, unsociological, account of ritual in Christianity, from the point of view of an author influenced by Zen and Taoism.

18. See G. Ryley Scott *Phallic Worship* (Luxor Press, London 1966). Also C. Jung *Man and His Symbols* (Aldus Books, London 1964).

19. *The Bible and the Beads* (Published by the London Committee for Walsingham). A way of saying the Rosary based on Scriptural passages, for Anglicans.

20. See D. Martin *Pacifism* (Routledge & Kegan Paul, London 1965).

21. See F. Parkin *Middle Class Radicalism* (Manchester University Press, 1968).

22. See C. Critcher, 'Football and Cultural Values' in *Working Papers in Cultural Studies* (University of Birmingham, spring 1971).

23. H. Gerth and C. W. Mills *From Max Weber* (Routledge & Kegan Paul, London 1948) see chapter IX 'The Sociology of Charismatic Authority'.

24. See M. Ramsey, Archbishop of Canterbury *Rome and Canterbury* (S.P.C.K., London 1967).

25. The Church Union, an Anglican Catholic group, rejected the scheme for Anglican Methodist Unity in 1968. Reasons are given by Bishop of Willesden in a pamphlet published by him in 1968 *To Every Man's Conscience* . . .

26. See M. Douglas *Purity and Danger. An Analysis of Concepts of Pollution and Taboo* (Routledge & Kegan Paul, London 1966).

27. See important sociological study of theology and management in the Church of England by P. F. Rudge *Ministry and Management* (Tavistock Publications, London 1968).

28. See B. Wilson *Religion in Secular Society* (C. A. Watts, London 1966) p. 11.

29. D. H. Morgan, 'The Social and Educational Background of Anglican Bishops—Continuities and Changes' in *British Journal of Sociology*, vol. XX, 1969, pp. 295-310.

30. See article by Sir John Lawrence in *Frontier*, August 1972.

31. Weber, op. cit. (note 8).

32. See B. Wilson *Religious Sects* (Weidenfeld & Nicolson, London 1970).

CHAPTER FIVE

1. See M. Fortes, 'Ritual and Office in Tribal Society' in M. Gluckman (ed.) *Essays on the Ritual of Social Relations* (Manchester University Press, 1962).

2. Report of the Archbishop's Commission—*Church and State* (Church Information Office, London 1970) quotation pp. 2-3.

3. E. Shils and M. Young, 'The Meaning of the Coronation' in *Sociological Review*, vol. I, 1953, pp. 63-81. Reprinted in S. Lipset and N. Smelser *Sociology. The Progress of a Decade* (Prentice-Hall, New Jersey 1961).

4. Shils and Young, op. cit.

5. See H. Frankel *Capitalist Society and Modern Sociology* (Lawrence & Wishart, London 1970).

6. These figures relate to 1960, and were published by *The Economist*, 15 January 1966.

7. See R. J. Bocock, 'Anglo-Catholic Socialism: A Study of a Protest Movement within a Church' in *Social Compass*, vol. XX, 1973.

8. The notion of 'legitimation' being used here is that of Max Weber. See H. Gerth and C. W. Mills *From Max Weber* (Routledge & Kegan Paul, London 1948) pp. 78-9 of 1970 paperback edition.

9. See here crucial passage in T. Parsons *The Structure of Social Action* (Free Press of Glencoe, New York 1949) chapter XVII, section on 'Legitimate Order, Charisma and Religion'.

10. See *New Society* survey 'Do We Want Our Children Taught About God?' in *New Society*, no. 139, 27 May 1965, pp. 8-10.

11. A good historical account of the Christian Socialists is J. Oliver *The Church and Social Order* (A. R. Mowbray & Co., London 1968).

Also see J. Klugman and P. Oestreicher *What Kind of Revolution? A Christian-Communist Dialogue* (Panther Books, London 1968).

12. For example, The Bishop of Liverpool reported in *The Guardian*, 11 February, 1972.

13. Diocesan Letter in a diocese under study for this research. April 1972.

14. Archbishop's Commission, op. cit. (note 2), chapter 3.

15. D. Martin *A Sociology of English Religion* (Heinemann, London 1967).

Also A. MacIntyre *Secularisation and Moral Change* (Oxford University Press, London 1967).

16. Archbishop's Commission, op. cit. (note 2). Memorandum of Dissent by Valerie Pitt.

17. Article by Trevor Huddleston, Bishop of Stepney, in *Sunday Times* 29 March 1972.

18. W. Lloyd Warner *American Life: Dream and Reality* (University of Chicago, 1953) quotation from chapter 1.

19. This poem by Wilfred Owen was used by Benjamin Britten in his *War Requiem*. See discussion of this work in Chapter Seven, 'Aesthetic Ritual'.

20. M. Eliade *Myths, Dreams and Mysteries* (France 1957; Harvill Press, London 1960).

21. Compare M. Gluckman *Custom and Conflict in Africa* (Blackwell, Oxford 1956 and 1970) chapter V, 'The Licence in Ritual'.

22. See E. Durkheim on 'Sacrifice' in Chapter Four of this book.

23. Eliade, op. cit. (note 20), quotation from p. 21 of 1970 Fontana edition.

CHAPTER SIX

1. For example, J. A. Robinson *Christian Freedom in a Permissive Society* (S.C.M. Press, London 1970).

Also D. R. Mace *The Christian Response to the Sexual Revolution* (Abingdon Press, U.S.A. 1970; Lutterworth Press, London 1971).

2. M. Mead *Male and Female* (Morrow, U.S.A. 1950; Pelican Books, Harmondsworth 1962).

3. For example, Y. Cohen *The Transition from Childhood to Adolescence* (Aldine Publishing Co., Chicago 1964).

B. Bettleheim *Symbolic Wounds, Puberty Rites and the Envious Male* (Free Press of Glencoe, New York 1954).

4. E. Durkheim *The Elementary Forms of the Religious Life* (Collier, U.S.A. 1961) book 3, chapter 1, section 2, contains descriptions of rites of initiation among Australian aborigines, which is a classic section in the literature on this topic.

5. M. Eliade *Myths, Dreams and Mysteries* (France 1957; Harvill Press, London 1960) quotation from p. 199 of the 1970 Fontana edition.

6. On the possible function of gang fighting in modern industrial societies as a form of male initiation rite, see J. Whiting, R. Kluckhon, A. Anthony, 'The Function of Male Initiation Ceremonies at Puberty', in E. Maccoby, T. Newcomb, E. Hartley (eds.) *Readings in Social Psychology* (Holt, New York 1958).

Critique of the approach used in the above: F. Young, 'The Function of Male Initiation Ceremonies: A Cross-Cultural Test of an Alternative Hypothesis' *American Journal of Sociology* 67, 1962, pp. 379-96.

Also F. Young, *Initiation Ceremonies: A Cross-Cultural Study of Status-Dramatisation* (Bobbs-Merrill, Indianapolis 1965).

7. W. Whyte *Street Corner Society: The Social Structure of an Italian Slum* (University of Chicago Press, 1943).

8. *King and Country*, directed by Joseph Losey, 1964.

9. See notes 20, 21, and 22 in Chapter Four of this book.

10. L. Tiger *Men in Groups* (Panther Books, London 1971).

11. See P. Willmot *Adolescent Boys of East London* (Routledge & Kegan Paul, London 1966).

12. A. van Gennep, *Rites de Passage* (Routledge & Kegan Paul, London 1960)

13. See discussion of A. Wallace on p. 54 of this book.

14. van Gennep, op. cit. (note 12).

See also M. Gluckman, 'Les Rites de Passage' in M. Gluckman *Essays on the Ritual of Social Relations* (Manchester University Press, 1962).

V. Turner *The Ritual Process* (Routledge & Kegan Paul, London 1969).

15. Gluckman, op. cit., quotation from p. 24.

16. M. Yinger *The Scientific Study of Religion* (Macmillan, New York 1970) p. 262.

17. In addition to Yinger, op. cit., see D. Martin, 'The Denomination', in *British Journal of Sociology*, vol. XIII, 1962.

18. Robinson, op. cit. (note 1), p. 149.

19. See references in note 17. Also W. Stark *Sociology of Religion. Established Religion* (Routledge & Kegan Paul, London 1967).

20. The Report of the Commission on Christian Initiation *Christian Initiation. Birth and Growth in the Christian Society* (Central Board of Finance of the Church of England, London 1971. For the Church of England Board of Education).

21. ibid., para. 99, p. 37.

22. B. Bernstein, 'A Socio-Linguistic Approach to Social Learning' in J. Gould (ed.) *Penguin Survey of the Social Sciences* (Penguin Books, Harmondsworth 1965).

23. ibid., para. 123, p. 42.

24. The Country Churchman—'Baptism'. Church Album no. 1, based on new 1967 service (The Abbey Press, Abingdon, Berks) quotation from p. 10.

25. On liminality see especially V. Turner *The Ritual Process* (Routledge & Kegan Paul, London 1969).

26. The Country Churchman, op. cit. (note 24).

27. ibid.

28. The Report of the Commission on Christian Initiation, op. cit. (note 20) para. 29, p. 34.

29. ibid., para. 67, p. 27.

30. ibid., para. 123, p. 42.

31. This information is up to 1967. Sources: Church Information Office: Facts and Figures about the Church of England. *Registrar General's Statistical Review*, 1967.

32. See article in *Time* Magazine, 23 August 1971.

33. Interview reported in *The Observer*, 23 January 1972.

34. See B. Wilson *Religion in Secular Society* (C. A. Watts, London 1966) pp. 65-7 documents the changes.

35. See C. Rodd, 'Church Affiliation and Denominational Values' in *Sociology*, vol. 2, no. 1, 1968, pp. 79-90.

36. See data reported in M. Schofield *The Sexual Behaviour of Young People* (Longmans, London 1965; revised edition, Pelican Books, Harmondsworth 1968).

37. Cf. Wilson, op. cit. (note 34) p. 70 of Watts edition.

38. See R. J. Bocock, 'The Role of the Anglican Clergyman' in *Social Compass*, vol. XVII, 1970, pp. 533-44.

39. See A. MacIntyre *Secularisation and Moral Change* (Oxford University Press, London 1967) chapter 1, p. 35 especially.

40. G. Gorer *Death, Grief and Mourning* (The Cresset Press, London 1965) see Table IV, p. 141.

41. See B. Martin, 'Comments on some Gallup Poll Statistics' in D. Martin (ed.) *Sociological Yearbook of Religion in Britain*, no. 1 (S.C.M. Press, London 1968) p. 154.

42. Gorer, op. cit. (note 40) p. 33.

43. ibid., p. 40.

44. Wilson, op. cit. (note 34) quotation on p. 71.

45. The need for this is argued at a theoretical level by P. Berger *The Social Reality of Religion* (Faber, London 1969) (Published in America in 1967, under the title *The Sacred Canopy*).

See also T. Luckman *The Invisible Religion* (Macmillan, New York 1967).

46. G. K. Nelson *Spiritualism and Society* (Routledge & Kegan Paul, London 1969).

Also B. Martin, 'The Spiritualist Meeting' in D. Martin and M. Hill (eds.) *Sociological Yearbook of Religion in Britain*, no. 3 (S.C.M. Press, London 1970).

47. Dom. R. Petitpierre, O.S.B. (ed.) *Exorcism* (S.P.C.K., London 1972).

48. Martin, op. cit. (note 41) p. 155.

49. Petitpierre, op. cit. (note 47) p. 17.

50. For a reductionist approach see G. Swanson *The Birth of the Gods: The Origins of Primitive Beliefs* (University of Michigan, Ann Arbor 1960).

51. Petitpierre, op. cit. (note 47) pp. 23-4.

52. C. Jung *Modern Man in Search of a Soul* (Routledge & Kegan Paul, London 1933; Routledge paperback 1961).

53. The Church of England Liturgical Commission *The Burial of the Dead* (S.P.C.K., London 1967).

54. ibid., pp. 11-13.

55. Benjamin Britten's *War Requiem* is discussed in Chapter Seven, 'Aesthetic Ritual' of this book.

56. M. Weber *The Sociology of Religion* (1922, German edition; 1963, Beacon Press, U.S.A.; 1965, Methuen, London, and as a Social Science Paperback, 1966) see pp. 103-8 of the latter edition.

57. ibid., p. 107.

CHAPTER SEVEN

1. See B. Wilson *Religion in Secular Society* (C. A. Watts, London 1966).

2. See the important historical and phenomenological study by Geradus van der Leeuw *Sacred and Profane Beauty: The Holy in Art* (Holt, Rinehart & Winston, U.S.A. 1963).

3. R. Williams, 'Literature and Sociology' in *New Left Review*, no. 67, 1971, p. 13.

4. See for example, B. Wicker *Culture and Liturgy* and T. Eagleton *The New Left Church* (Sheed & Ward, London 1966).

5. A. Goldman and E. Sprinchorn *Wagner on Music and Drama* (Gollancz, London 1964 and 1970) p. 60.

6. van der Leeuw, op. cit. (note 2) p. 97 of paperback edition.

7. R. Mander and J. Mitchenson *British Music Hall* (Studio Vista, London 1965).

8. For some idea of Peter Brook's methods of direction and views on theatre, see his *The Empty Space* (MacGibbon & Kee, London 1968).

For discussion of experimental methods in theatre with special references to ritual, see J. Roose-Evans *Experimental Theatre. From Stanislavsky to Today* (Universe Books, New York 1970).

See also J. Goodlad *A Sociology of Popular Drama* (Heinemann, London 1971) chapter 1 on 'The Association of Drama with Ritual'.

9. I. Stravinsky *Poetics of Music in the Form of Six Lessons* (1942 Copyright; Harvard University Press, U.S.A. 1970).

10. B. Britten *War Requiem* (Decca Record Company, London 1963).

11. See N. O. Brown *Life against Death* (Wesleyan University, U.S.A. 1959; Sphere Books, London 1968) quotation p. 84 of the latter edition.

12. Recent recording of *Parsifal* with Pierre Boulez conducting, Bayreuth, 1970 (Deutsche Grammophon, 1971).

13. A. Wallace *Religion: An Anthropological View* (Random House, New York 1966).

14. *Jesus Christ, Superstar* (Leeds Music Ltd, 1970; M.C.A. Records, New York).

15. Source: clergy interviews carried out by author, 1971.

16. M. Eliade *Myth and Reality* (George Allen & Unwin, London 1964).

17. W. O. E. Oesterley *The Sacred Dance* (Cambridge University Press, 1923).

18. van der Leeuw, op. cit. (note 2) pp. 54-5 of paperback edition (Abingdon Press, New York 1963).

19. See J. Percival *Modern Ballet* (Studio Vista, London 1970).

20. F. Rust *Dance and Society* (Routledge & Kegan Paul, London 1969). Contains some empirical material on dance and dancing among young British people in the 1960s.
More journalistic is G. Melly *Revolt into Style. The Pop Arts in Britain* (Allen Lane, The Penguin Press, London 1970).

21. Interviews conducted by author. For literature on working-class self-identification see J. Goldthorpe *et al.* *The Affluent Worker in the Class Structure* vol. 3 (Cambridge University Press, 1969).

22. B. Jackson *Working Class Community* (Routledge & Kegan Paul, London 1968) quotation from p. 38 of 1972 Pelican edition.

23. S. Langer *Philosophy in a New Key* (Harvard University Press, 1943) see especially chapter 8 'On Significance in Music'.

24. C. Critcher, 'Football and Cultural Values' in *Working Papers in Cultural Studies* (University of Birmingham Press, spring 1971).

25. See for similar argument, E. Fisher *The Necessity of Art. A Marxist Approach* (Penguin Books, Harmondsworth 1963).

26. L. A. Fielder *The Return of the Vanishing American* (Jonathan Cape, London 1968).
P. Woolen *Signs and Meaning on the Cinema* (Secker & Warburg, London 1969; second edition Thames & Hudson, London 1970).
I. Butler *Religion in the Cinema* (A. S. Barnes, New York and A. Zwemmer London 1969).

CHAPTER EIGHT

1. This is a useful concept in this context, the usage being similar to that of T. Roszak in his *The Making of a Counter-Culture* (Faber, London 1968 and 1970).

2. See, for example, W. Hedgepeth & D. Stock *The Alternative Communal Life in New America* (Macmillan Company, N.Y. 1970).
Also O. Klapp *The Collective Search for Identity* (Holt, Rinehart & Winston, U.S.A. 1969).

3. See J. Needleman *The New Religions* (Doubleday, N.Y. 1970; and Pocket Books, N.Y. 1972).

4. A. Etzioni uses the term calculative involvement to characterise a type of involvement in modern complex organisations in his *A Comparative Analysis of Complex Organisations* (Free Press of Glencoe, New York 1961).

5. J. Habermas *Toward a Rational Society* (Suhrkamp Verlag, Frankfurt am Main 1968; Heinemann Educational Books, London 1971) pp. 121-2.

6. See the conclusion to J. Ben-David *The Scientist's Role in Society* (Prentice-Hall, N.Y. and London 1971).

7. M. Gluckman *Custom and Conflict in Africa* (Blackwell, Oxford 1956 and 1970). See especially Chapter V, 'The Licence in Ritual'.

8. J. L. Peacock *The Rites of Modernisation: Symbolic and Social Aspects of Indonesian Proletarian Drama* (University of Chicago Press, 1968). Good example of a recent attempt to study change.

Also M. Wilson *Religion and the Transformation of Society* (Cambridge University Press, 1971). Study of change in traditional ritual in Africa and the influence of Christianity.

9. W. Pahnke, 'L.S.D. and Religious Experience' in R. C. deBold and R. Leaf (eds.) *L.S.D., Man and Society* (Faber, London 1961) p. 77.

10. See R. Bendix *Max Weber. An Intellectual Portrait* (Heinemann, London 1960).

11. See H. Marcuse *An Essay on Liberation* (Beacon Press, U.S.A.; Allen Lane, The Penguin Press, London 1969). Especially Chapter II, 'The New Sensibility'.

12. F. Parkin *Class Inequality and Political Order* (MacGibbon & Kee, London 1971).

13. See L. Tiger *Men in Groups* (Thomas Nelson, London 1969). Especially Chapter One, 'Biology and the Study of Human Behaviour'.

14. N. O. Brown *Life Against Death* (Wesleyan University, U.S.A. 1959; Sphere Books, London 1969) quotation from p. 19 of the latter edition.

15. ibid., p. 61.

16. See C. Levi-Strauss *The Savage Mind* (France 1962; Weidenfeld & Nicolson, London 1966) chapter 9, 'History and Dialectic'.

17. See V. Turner *The Ritual Process* (Routledge & Kegan Paul, London 1969). An interesting attempt to study rituals among the Ndembu in Zambia.

18. J. Israel *Alienation. From Marx to Modern Sociology* (Allyn & Bacon Inc., Boston 1971) quotation from p. 39.

19. See E. Fischer *The Necessity of Art. A Marxist Approach* (Penguin Books, Harmondsworth 1963).

20. M. Eliade *Myths, Dreams and Mysteries* (Harvill Press, London 1960) quotation from p. 38 of Fontana edition, 1968.

21. K. Marx *Economic and Philosophic Manuscripts of 1844* (Lawrence & Wishart, London 1959).

22. On role of artists see T. Parsons *The Social System* (Routledge & Kegan Paul, London 1951) chapter IX.

23. *Newsweek Review*, 5 June 1972, p. 56.

24. P. Brook *The Empty Space* (MacGibbon & Kee, London 1968) quotation from chapter II, p. 67 of Pelican edition.

25. T. O'Dea *The Mormons* (University of Chicago Press, 1957), and see also B. Wilson *Religious Sects* (Weidenfeld & Nicolson, London 1970).

26. Classical statement of key ideas in this area can be found in Maxwell Jones *Social Psychiatry in Practice. The Idea of the Therapeutic Community* (Penguin Books, Harmondsworth 1968).

27. The potential bibliography here is large. Key ideas can be found in the following:

A. Lowen *The Betrayal of the Body* (Macmillan Company, U.S.A. 1967).

R. D. Laing *The Politics of Experience* (Penguin Books, Harmondsworth 1967).

F. Perls, R. Hefferline, P. Goodman *Gestalt Therapy* (Dell Publishing Co., New York 1951).

28. J. Young *The Drugtakers. The Social Meaning of Drug Use* (MacGibbon & Kee, London 1971) see p. 126 of Paladin edition.

D. Matza and G. Sykes *Juvenile Delinquency and Subterranean Values* in *American Sociological Review*, no. 26, p. 716.

29. See for example, T. Parsons *Structure and Process in Modern Societies* (Frank Cass, London 1960) and *The Social System*, op. cit. (note 22).

30. The work of the Centre for Contemporary Cultural Studies, University of Birmingham, which produces a publication 'Working Papers in Cultural Studies', has carried out the most interesting research here.

See also J. Nuttall *Bomb Culture* (MacGibbon & Kee, London 1968).

31. See Young, op. cit. (note 28).

32. D. Cooper *The Death of the Family* (A. Lane, London 1971). Written as a result of work and experiences in a communal situation in London.

33. See J. Mitchell *Woman's Estate* (Penguin Books, Harmondsworth 1966 and 1971).

G. Greer *The Female Eunuch* (MacGibbon & Kee, London 1970).

D. Teal *The Gay Militants* (Stein & Day, New York 1971).

34. P. Hollander *American and Soviet Society* (Prentice-Hall, Englewood Cliffs 1969). Paper on 'Reflections on Soviet Juvenile Delinquency'.

35. J. Robinson *The Cultural Revolution in China* (Penguin Books, Harmondsworth 1969).

36. H. Gerth and C. W. Mills *From Max Weber. Essays in Sociology* (Routledge & Kegan Paul, London 1948) chapter XIII.

37. On typology of attitudes to nature, and others, see F. Kluckhohn and F. Strodtbeck *Variations in Value Orientations* (Harper & Row, N.Y. 1961).

Index